New Books • Special Offers • Diary • Workshops • For

Worth reading!

The newsletter of the *Therapy Book Club* **October 2003**

ALL PRICES FEATURED REPRESENT A GREATER DISCOUNT THAN MEMBERS' STANDARD 5%

New books

NEW
Loss and Learning Disability
Noelle Blackman
£16.99 ***TBC £15.50***

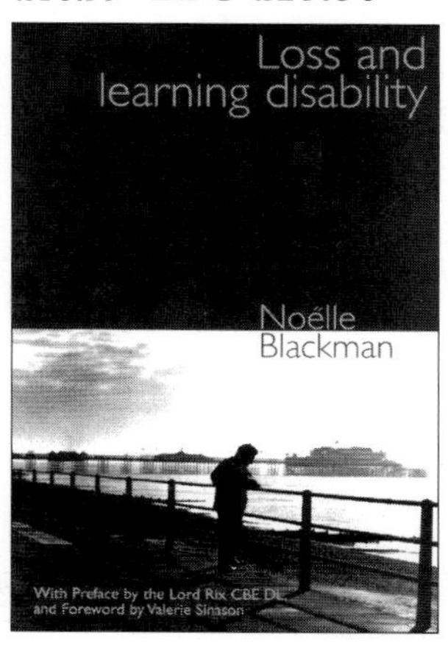

The emotional life of people with learning disabilities is a subject that has only begun to be thought about during the last decade. This important book addresses the central issue of how people with learning disabilities can be affected by loss and bereavement.

The author draws on her extensive clinical experience of working with people with learning disabilities who have often been left alone to struggle with the pain of loss and bereavement.

Accessible, impassioned and highly informative, the book includes pro-active strategies to prevent grief complications, and therapeutic interventions for helping people when the grief process "goes wrong. Of benefit to those working directly with people with learning disabilities, as well as to those who wish to extend their practice to offer therapy or counselling to this group of people.

"A moving, rigorous and erudite book. It is a feast... to make something so unbearable so approachable is a real testimony to Noelle Blackman's clinical and writing skills".

Foreword by Valerie Sinason

Preface by Lord Brian Rix

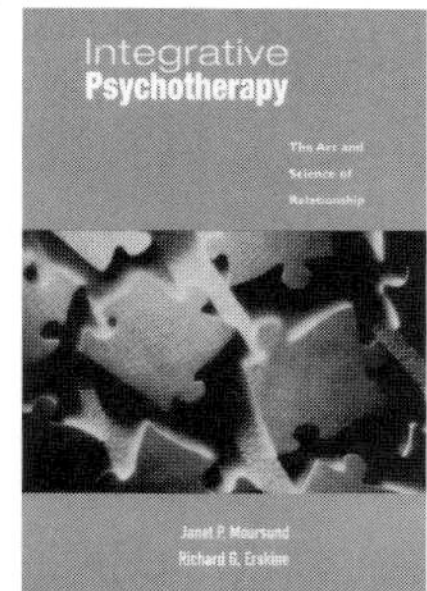

NEW **Integrative Psychotherapy: The Art and Science of Relationship**
Janet P. Moursurd & Richard G. Erskine
£24.99
TBC £21.99

Superbly researched and written, familiar topics presented in a new manner.

NEW
Embodied Psychotherapist: The Therapist's Body Story
Robert Shaw
£16.99
TBC £14.99

A potentially valuable description and exploration of the ways practitioners use their bodily feelings within the therapeutic encounter.

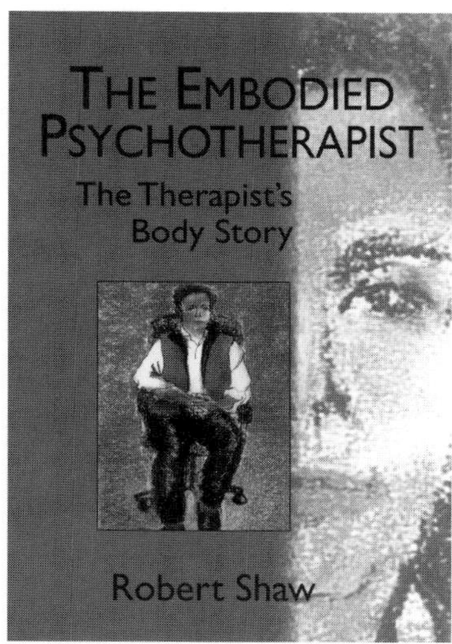

Therapist as Life Coach: Transforming Your Practice
Patrick Williams & Deborah C. Davis
£25.00
TBC £22.50

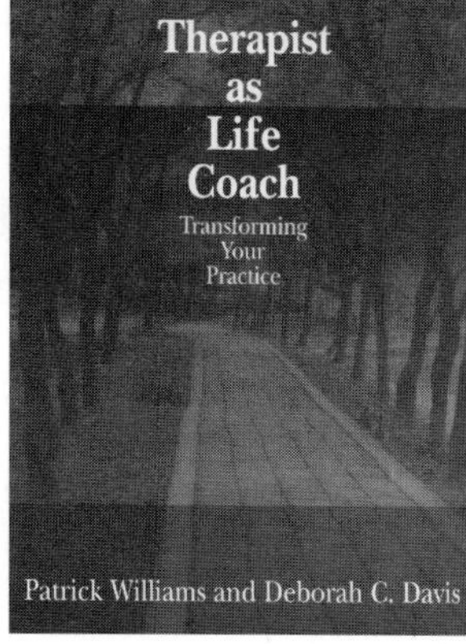

Life coaching (or personal coaching) is the second biggest consulting industry after management consulting. Therapists are the professionals best positioned to move into this rapidly growing field: they are experts at listening, encouraging and facilitating change. Coaching allows therapists to use their current training with a wide population of clients, who seek to maximize their life potential. This book is one-stop shopping for the therapist wishing to explore the coaching field.

NEW **The Little Book of Procrastination**
Andrea Perry
£2.99 ***TBC £2.50***

A little book full of thoughts and images to get you going – finish that accreditation form/ dissertation/ life re-vamp today! ★ **Stocking filler** ★

E-mail

We are increasing using e-mail as a way of quickly communicating good offers to members. If you have not received any e-mails from us this year, and would like to, please e-mail us at andrea@worth reading.demon.co.uk, with the header, "Newsletter". Thanks.

To order: telephone 020 7289 5677 fax 020 7289 5672
Why not come and see us? (nearest tube, Maida Vale on the Bakerloo line)

6 Lauderdale Parade, London W9 1LU 020 7289 5677 ap@worthreading.demon.co.uk. www.worthreading.co.uk

Race and Culture

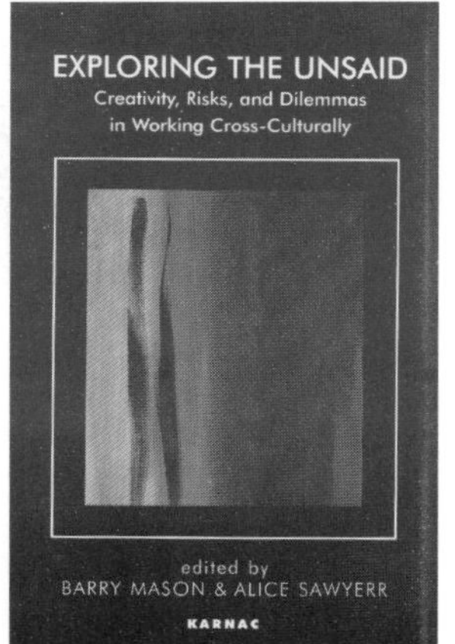

Exploring the Unsaid: Creativity, Risks, and Dilemmas in Working Cross-Culturally
Barry Mason & Alice Sawyer
£19.99 ***TBC £17.99***
Formulates a thoughtful and innovative framework for progress in this complex and demanding field – addresses 'sameness' and 'difference', 'collectivism' and 'individualism', internalised and institutionalised racism, and much more. ★ **Reading list** ★

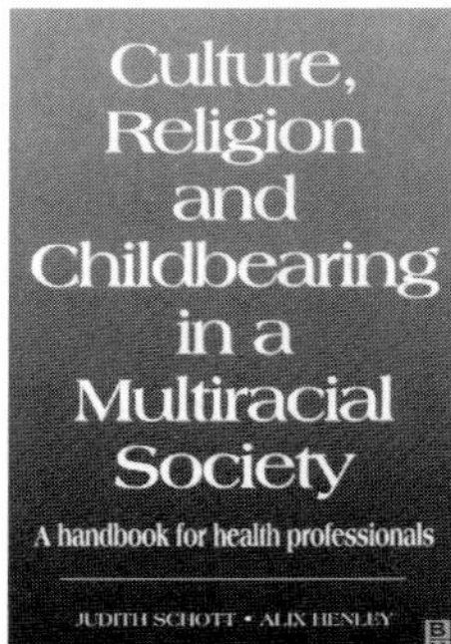

Culture, Religion and Childbearing in a Multiracial Society
Judith Schott & Alix Hensley
£21.99 ***TBC £18.99***
Presents down-to-earth, practical and constructive ways of enhancing practice. Gentle and challenging; for those involved in planning or providing women's health services.

Racial Identity, White Counsellors and Therapists
Gillian Tuckwell
£16.99 ***TBC £14.99***
Writing from an integrative perspective, the author challenges white therapists to be aware of what it means to be white, and how this influences the therapy process.

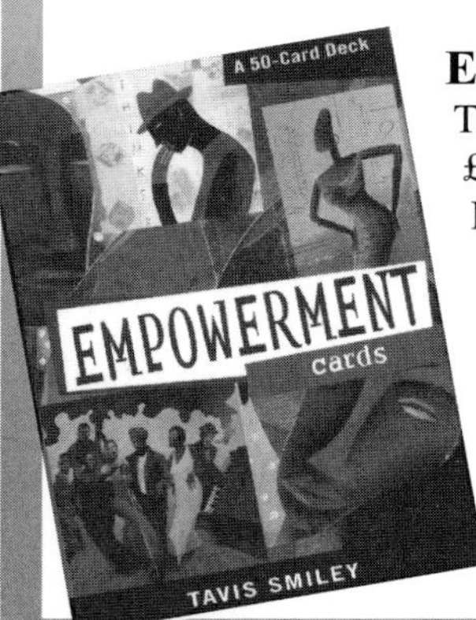

Empowerment cards
Tavis Smiley
£11.99 ***TBC £9.99***
Multi-purpose well presented box of cards with multi-cultural images and genuinely empowering messages: *defy the fear – change your internal chit-chat – say thanks in advance – appreciate the obstacle – embrace authenticity.*
For adolescents and adults.

Family

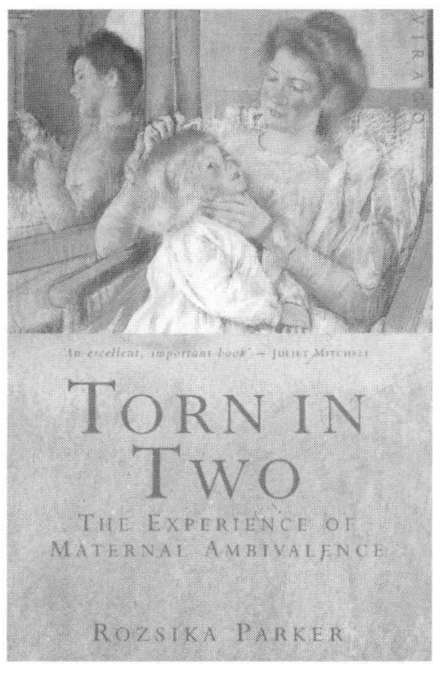

Torn in Two – the Experience of Maternal Ambivalence
Rozsika Parker
£10.99 ***TBC £11.50***
"A major and novel contribution to our understanding of the complexities of motherhood with implications that branch out in many directions. An excellent, important book".
Juliet Mitchell.

Inconceivable Conceptions: Psychological Aspects of Infertility and Reproductive Technology
Edited by Jane Haynes & Juliet Miller
£16.99 ***TBC £14.99***
Examines the experience of infertility from both female and male perspectives, as well as the psychological aspects of infertility diagnosis and treatment, and the unexpected effects on changing patterns of kinship.

Puppet offer!

-15% off all puppets until 31/12/03
(subject to stock availability)
- **Small: lions, chicks, racoon, elephant, bear, tortoise, witch, bunny, guinea-pig**
- **Big: dog, orang-utang, monkeys, shark, snake, black bear, crocodile. Learn new ways to use puppets with Holly Dwyer at *Worth reading!* on December 10**

Call us for more details.
Phone to check latest stock 020 7289 5677

Students' Mental Health Needs - Problems and responses
Eds. Nicky Stanley & Jill Manthorpe
£16.95 ***TBC £14.95***
Contributors examine how campus based agencies can work with the voluntary sector, community practitioners and students' families to provide effective support for students with mental health problems. The discussion is placed in the context of structural and economic changes in education and society, looking at the impact of family relationships, debt and financial difficulties, drug and alcohol abuse and academic challenges.

DIARY DATES: *Worth reading!* Bookstall conference + training programme November & De

November 1: Gestalt at Metanoia Institute, London. 1st year students, Institute of Arts in Therapy, London
November 3: Working with the families of people with mental illnesses, Institute of Family Therapy, London
November 8: The Wild Child: Genes? ADHD? Trauma? Parenting Problems? Just plain defiant? with Terry Levy, and Sue Jenner Centre for Child Mental Health, London
November 14: Eating Disorders Institute of Family Therapy, London
November 15: Dramatherapy, Play Therapy, Dance Movement Therapy at Roehampton Institute, London
November 17: Life Transitions Institute of Family Therapy, London
November 25: First in Class – last in li with Oliver James, Caspari Foundation Fu Raising Lecture, London
November 26: Learning Disability Exhibition, Business Design Centre, Islington, London
November 28: Systemic work in Organisations, Institute of Family Therapy, London

Matters

NEW The Importance of Sibling Relationships in Psychoanalysis

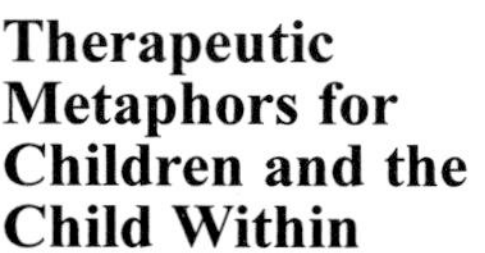

Prophecy Coles
£12.99
TBC £10.99

"A refreshingly new look into the world of sibling relationships, and how these can profoundly colour emotional development and subsequent relationships. It represents a challenge to all of us .. to notice the evidence and impact of sibling transference in our clinical work". Patrick Casement ★ **Intriguing** ★

NEW Parenting a child with Asperger syndrome – 200 tips and strategies
Brenda Boyd
£13.95 ***TBC £11.95***
A refreshing approach – easy to read, practical and realistic.

Dangerous Encounters - Avoiding Perilous Situations with Autism
Bill Davis & Wendy Goldband Schunick
£13.95 ***TBC £11.99***

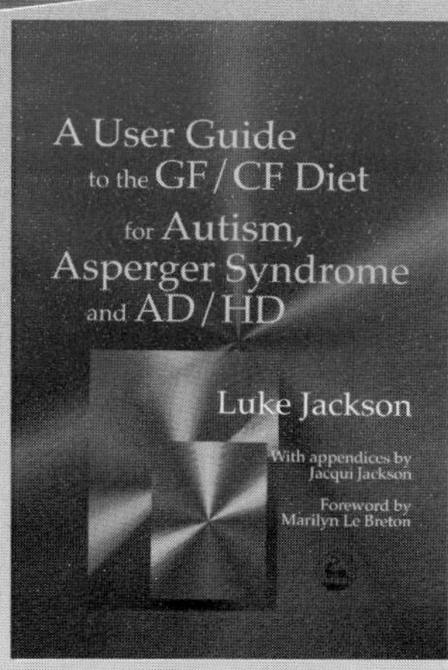

A User Guide to the GF/CF Diet for Autism, Asperger Syndrom and AD/HD
Luke Jackson
£12.95 ***TBC £11.50***

NEW Parenting and Disability: Disabled parents' experiences of raising children
Richard Olsen & Harriet Clark, £18.99 ***TBC £16.99***
Reports on the first substantial UK study of parenting, disability and mental health, reviewing policy issues, barriers to full participation that disabled parents face, and advocates ways of supporting disabled parents and their families. Well-researched and constructive.

Therapeutic Metaphors for Children and the Child Within
Joyce Mills & Richard J. Crowley
£26.95 ***TBC £24.50***
Creative clinicians present innovative methods in an eminently understandable and readable fashion – usable with children of all ages.
★ **Reading list** ★

NEW I'm Bored! Over 100 inspiring and imaginative ideas for hours of fun with your children Suzy Barrat & Polly Beard
£7.99 ***TBC £6.99***
Indispensable selection of fun and original ideas to amuse and enthuse children of all ages – at home, indoors, outdoors, while travelling, or even at the beach.
★ **Ages 3 - 85 Imaginative** ★

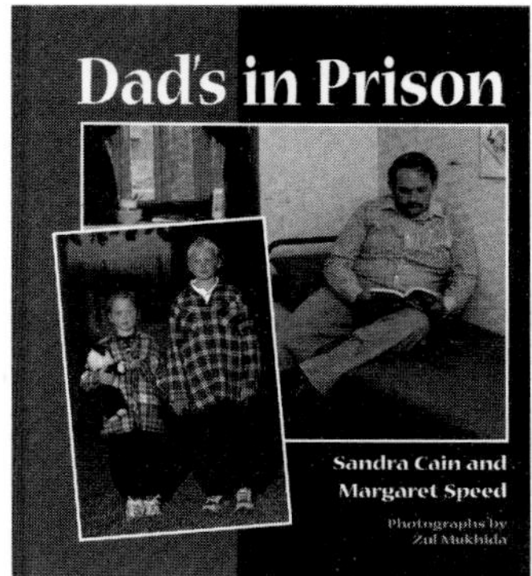

Dad's in Prison
Sandra Cain & Margaret Speed
£8.99 ***TBC £6.99***

Increasing Competence through Collaborative Problem-Solving
Gerda Hanko
£18.00
TBC £15.99

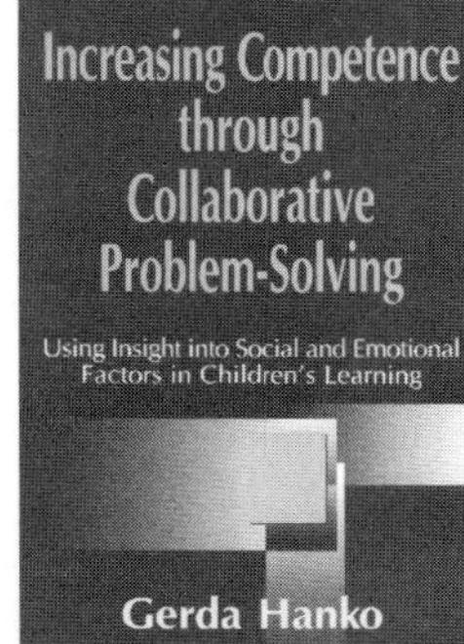

Imprisoned Fathers and their children
Gwyneth Boswell & Peter Wedge
£15.95 ***TBC £13.99***
An useful resource for all those working with the families of fathers in prison.

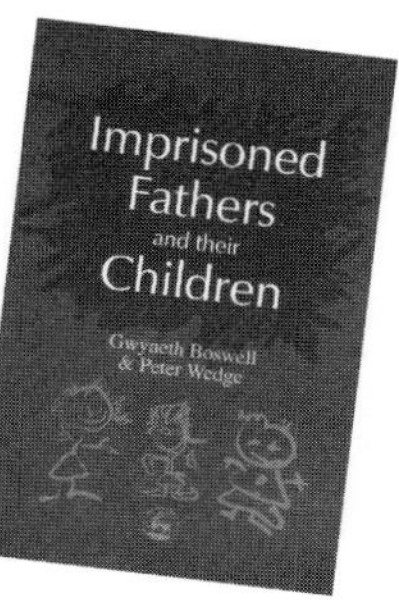

...ber 2003

November 29: BACP Counselling in Education London
December 5: Re-writing Scripts, Institute of Family Therapy, London
December 6: From Counsellor to Coach – crossing the bridge successfully. *A Masterclass with Michael Carroll Ph.D* London
December 13: 1st year students, Institute of Arts in Therapy, London

Attachment and the Brain

Attachment Theory, Child Maltreatment and Family Support
David Howe, Marian Brandon, Diana Hinings & Gillian Schofield
£16.99 ***TBC £14.99***
Ground breaking text offers a comprehensive account of how social developmental perspectives and attachment theory can guide practice in child welfare, family support, adoption etc.
★ **Practitioner recommended** ★

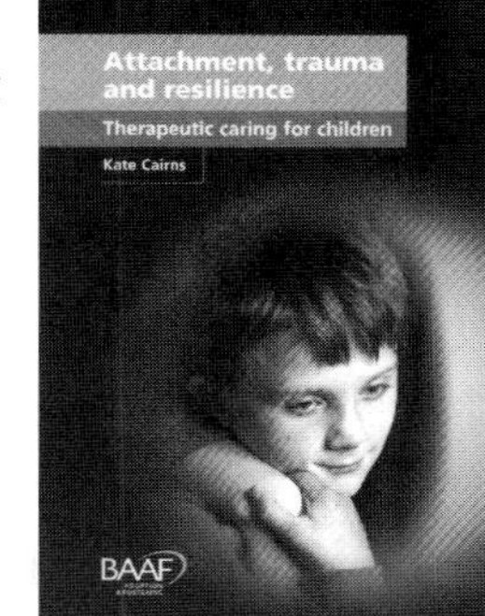

Attachment, trauma and resilience: Therapeutic caring for children
Kate Cairns
£9.95 ***TBC £8.95***
Professional and personal experiences of family life with children who have lived through overwhelming stress. Identifies what can be done to promote recovery and resilience.
★ **Practitioner recommended** ★

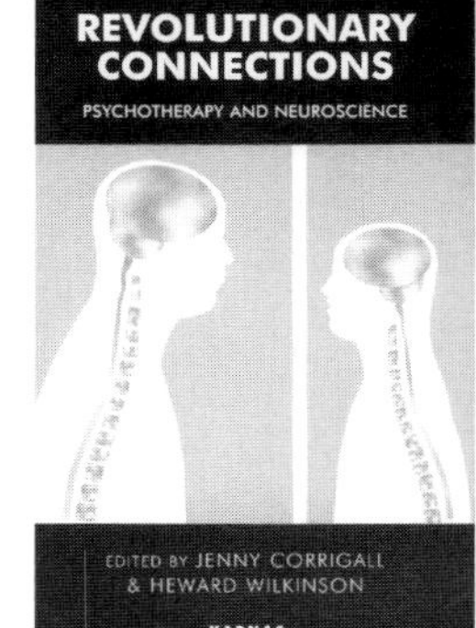

Revolutionary Connections: Psychotherapy and Neuroscience
Jenny Corrigale & Heward Wilkinson
£19.99 ***TBC £17.99***
Collection of practical and theoretical articles based on the 2001 UKCP conference on this theme.

The Brain and the Inner World: An introduction to the neuroscience of subjective experience
Mark Solms & Oliver Turnbull
£18.99
TBC £15.99
A readable introduction to the intimate relationship between neuroscience and analysis/therapy.

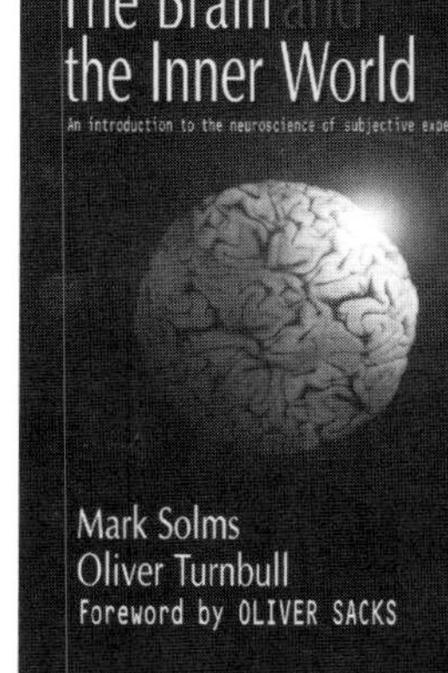

Therapy Book Club Author Events

Which books have influenced you most professionally? Which books do you find yourself recommending to colleagues? Which authors would you most like to meet to exchange ideas stimulated by their writing?
Let us know which authors have made a significant impact on your thinking and practice, and we may able to organise an AUTHOR EVENT.
Following the successful day with Dr. Karl-Heinz Brisch (see panel), we are delighted to offer a workshop with **Dr. Jenifer Elton-Wilson**, author of "Time-Conscious Psychological Therapy: a life stage to go through" (Routledge 1996) on her forthcoming work (with Gabrielle Syme) on "Outcomes and Objectives".

Workshop: THE IMPOSSIBLE ENTERPRISE? An exploration of the effective use of objectives and outcomes in therapy, looking at the purposes and consequences of therapy for client, practitioner, the immediate social system and for society at large.

Date: January 17th 2004
Time: 9.30 - 12.30pm
Cost: £36 (TBC £29.00, with additional £5 discount for booking before 15/12/03
Venue: London (nr. Euston Station)

For more details or to reserve a place, contact 020 7289 5677 or see www.worthreading.co.uk <http://www.worthreading.co.uk> (Author Events)

Comments on the last Author Event with Dr. Karl-Heinz Brisch, author of **Treating Attachment Disorders** (18.10.03)
"Brilliant day. Having the author present brings their world so much more alive, with the opportunity to dialogue and explore". "Made the whole concept of attachment easy to understand". "Informative and thought-provoking – a very worthwhile day".
Dr Brisch will return in May 2004 – contact us for more details

For those who missed this stimulating day (and videos), why not read the book?
Treating Attachment Disorders
£26.95
TBC £24.90

HOW TO FIND US

N
Maida Vale (Edgware Road) → West End
Maida Vale (Bakerloo Line)
Elgin Avenue
Lauderdale Road
Worth reading!
Sutherland Avenue
No 6 bus
Shirland Road → West End
No 6 bus

ALL OFFERS EXPIRE 31/12/03
and are subject to availability.

FREE POSTAGE
on orders over £40

We are now offering FREE POSTAGE on any single order worth £40 or more.

For smaller orders, postage will be:
Retail value:
£0 - £19.99: **£2.60** • £20 - £39.99: **£3.95.**
We hope this makes life simpler!

All items will be sent 2nd class.
Effective 19th May 2003.

Worth reading!© is the newsletter of the ***Worth reading!*** Therapy Book Club. All rights retained.
Worth reading! bookshop is at **6 Lauderdale Parade, London W9 1LU 020 7289 5677**
ap@worthreading.demon.co.uk. www.worthreading.co.uk

Therapeutic Groupwork with Children

Therapeutic Groupwork with Children

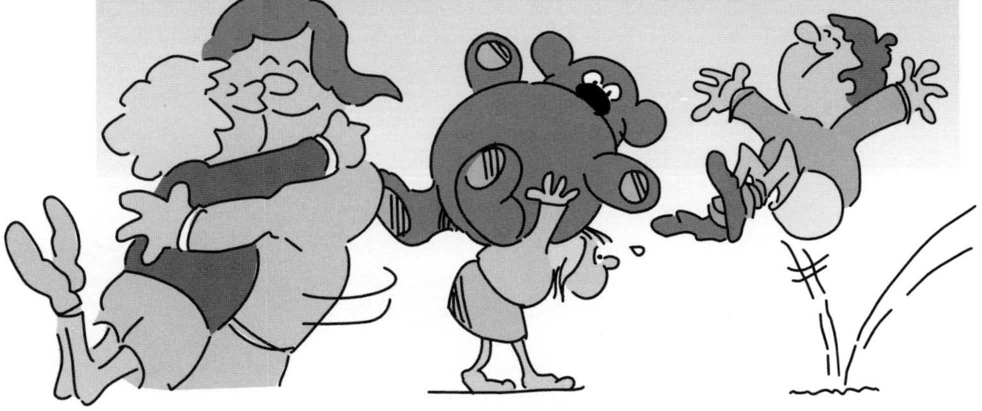

Joost Drost & Sydney Bayley

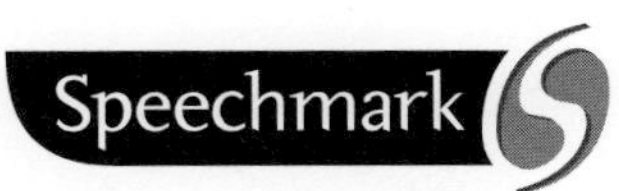

Speechmark Publishing Ltd
Telford Road, Bicester, Oxon OX26 4LQ, UK

PLEASE NOTE THAT IN THIS TEXT 'HE' IS USED TO REFER TO THE CHILD FOR THE SAKE OF CLARITY ALONE.

Published by
Speechmark Publishing Ltd, Telford Road, Bicester, Oxon OX26 4LQ, United Kingdom
Telephone: +44 (0)1869 244644   Fax: +44 (0)1869 320040
www.speechmark.net

First published 2001
Reprinted 2002, 2003

002-4255/Printed in the United Kingdom/1010

British Library Cataloguing in Publication Data

Drost, Joost
Therapeutic Groupwork with Children
1. Group psychotherapy for children – Great Britain – Handbooks, manuals, etc.
2. Occupational therapy for children – Great Britain
I.Title II. Bayley, Sydney
618.9'289152

ISBN 0 86388 234 X

CONTENTS

A word of thanks!

We are especially grateful to all the boys and girls who have participated in our groups and helped to develop our work. We must also thank their parents and teachers who gave us their trust.

We would not have been able to write this book without the support of our Child & Adolescent Directorate (North East Essex Mental Health Trust, Colchester) and especially the help of the secretaries, the trainee psychologists and Clare Hayward, Assistant Clinical Psychologist.

John McFayden has given us invaluable advice on how to develop our groups.

Kingsford Junior School in Colchester has been helpful in piloting the use of this book in schools. Their special needs coordinator, Frances Sheppard, and Sophie Doswell, Louise Candy and Kevin Beardsworth, all Clinical Psychologists in training, have given us encouraging feedback on how they were able to use the book.

We would like to see this book as a starting point, rather than a completed product. This can only be done with your help and your feedback, as well as further contributions.

At the end of this book you will find an invitation to help us.

We would therefore also like to thank you for participating, by reading, exploring and developing the thoughts and materials in this book.

Introduction

Our aim in writing this book has been to share with other professionals the work that we have been doing, within the context of a Child & Family Consultation Service, to develop methods and resources which might be helpful in building up the social, emotional and interpersonal skills of children, in the primary age range in general and specifically those who are experiencing behavioural difficulties. Our view is that this work can take place in Child Mental Health Clinics but also in schools and other settings.

We have worked with groups of children over a limited period in a therapeutic out-patient setting, but we can see the book being used quite flexibly, for example, in providing activities for Circle Time (Moseley, 1996).

Through using this book, we not only want you to be able to use the activities described, as you would with a cookbook, but hope that we can convey our underlying approach. In this way it might become an approach throughout the whole school, as mental health cannot simply be captured in activities: it is a climate!

The materials in this book have been developed over a period of four years with fourteen groups of boys (three of which also contained girls) aged 5 to 7, and 8 to 11. All of the children had been referred to the Child & Family Consultation Service. We started off with homogeneous groups, either consisting of aggressive children or those who were more likely to find themselves as victims, but we moved on to form groups with mixed difficulties.

Throughout the book, we refer to the client group as 'he' and many of the activities are orientated towards boys. This is because the vast majority of referrals by our colleagues to the groups have been boys, most of them with problems of self-control. Sometimes we had one referral of a girl for a particular group, but did not include her because we did not feel it would be fair to have one girl in a group with five boys. Recently, in order to accommodate more children with difficulties at the other end of the acting out/withdrawn spectrum and also to include more girls, whose needs may not be being met, we have changed our criteria for inclusion in our groups, so that we now take only two children with extreme acting out behaviour and we will reserve two places for girls. This will almost certainly necessitate adaptations to the activities and the introduction of new ones. We run ten session groups so that the life of the group can fit into one school term.

The way we work with groups is based on a world-view, a life philosophy, as this is the way most schools are run. In Chapter 1 we outline the basic principles through which we approach and understand the children, as well as the world around them. In Chapter 2 the role of the therapists or facilitators is explored, looking back on our own experiences on this steep learning curve.

For our first group we developed a series of activities, centred around certain themes, which are explained more fully in Chapter 3 and we have continued to refine these, add further activities or change the order, depending on the needs of a particular group.

A group is not a world in itself; it is a small moment in a child's life, a small window in a large world. In Chapter 4 we explore how the group fits in with school and families, and how the activities and approach can be transferred to other settings. In Chapter 5 we give a very brief overview of the theoretical background for working with groups of young children.

Part II contains the actual activities that we have designed for groups of children aged 5 to 7. These are ordered in the ten-session format, but we use a pick-and-mix approach, in order to tailor the programme to the needs of the group. For that reason we have added a note to each activity, stating its basic themes. Children aged 8 to 11 will benefit from a slightly different approach. Part II gives some guidelines for running the older groups and also gives an example of a ten-session programme with activities geared to this age group.

Reading this book will probably trigger as many questions as it answers. In this way the book is just a snapshot in time. We hope to develop our work further, both in our clinic setting and with schools. Part III encourages you to make up your own activities and gives you some guidelines.

We would welcome your feedback. We have already collected more activities and would like to invite all of you to send us your activities. In this way we hope to develop a database, to help support teachers in making mental health and personal growth an integral part of school life.

Part I

CHAPTER 1

The Colour of our Glasses: How we see the World

Perceptions and beliefs

Everything we do is guided by what we see, hear, taste and sense; by our perceptions and by the sense we make of these perceptions, whether it is how we walk and talk, how we relate to others, how we develop a course or how we manage a school.

These perceptions and the processes by which we make sense of them (our cognitions) can be influenced by putting on different types of glasses.

- Dark glasses can make a sunny world look pretty dull, even grim.
- Experiencing near dehydration in a desert can make the sun seem pretty hostile. You would like to hide.
- Living in Britain for most of your life can make the sun look like a treasure. You would like to embrace it.

The colour of our glasses is formed by our experiences and they will colour our future experiences. However, every experience will again influence the colour of our glasses, either confirming and re-enforcing, or challenging and changing, our basic beliefs.

This means that the way we approach others with whom we share the experiences will, in the end, help to build their basic beliefs, their future way of experiencing.

Groups and schools are an important experience for all those involved. The basic belief underlying our approach to running groups with children is: *there is a core part in every individual which is striving towards health and healing*.

We do recognise how difficult this may be to keep hold of within certain environments, but this core part of an individual can be appealed to and utilised in trying to bring about change. Children will generally respond positively when they feel they are listened to, accepted and valued. Under these conditions they are willing to question themselves and to learn. Where there has been a lot of damage to the child's self-esteem, this approach can take some time to have an effect, but we believe that it is the right one, both ethically and psychologically.

Children with behavioural difficulties have often developed faulty perceptions that determine the way they behave in certain situations. For example, a child who has learned from his experiences of the world that people tend to criticise him, may, when observing two children laughing in the playground, believe that they are laughing at him; the reality may be that they are sharing a joke, but by the time this becomes clear, a fight could have taken place. We believe that faulty perceptions are learned and thus can be unlearned, given the right setting. We hope to challenge these perceptions and try to provide alternative explanations of what might be happening when they seem to be operating within the group. We also use role-play activities which help the children to consider alternatives for themselves.

Awareness in the present

Also central to our thinking, is the belief that mental health starts with responding to what is happening in the present, rather than reacting from a place within ourselves that is influenced by what has happened to us in the past. A genuine dialogue between adult and adult, or adult and child, will start from this point and give both the feeling of having control over their lives.

Most of the children coming to our service have behavioural difficulties. They are not able to control their tempers. And what is our response as adults? When they are angry, we tell them to shut up and go to their room. We will take control, so who needs control? They protest as they lose their grip on the world around them. We pin them down and corner them even more. They then make desperate attempts to retain control of the tiniest piece of the world they can claim for themselves, their food, their room, the clothes they wear, their own thoughts.

We believe that, for many of the children we see, the locus of control has not been internalised and they see control as residing in others; usually the adults in their lives. This could be either because the adults have been over-controlling, or it could be that there has been inadequate control, leading the child to seek it desperately from others so that they can feel more secure. An important part of the group process revolves around trying to facilitate change, by encouraging the children to think about their behaviour in the present and to exercise more self-control. We do this through specific activities and through the way we facilitate the group from moment to moment, giving continuous open feedback (Chapter 2). At the beginning of each session we also give the children positive feedback about their behaviour in the previous session.

We consciously refrain from over-controlling the group by planning a very loose programme and giving time and attention to what happens at the time. We know, from others' work with groups, that individuals will bring their internal conflicts and social expectations to a group setting and act them out. We are prepared for this to happen and welcome it as material which we can attempt to make sense of, for ourselves, and then for the children.

Information processing and engraining

If we become stuck in life, it is important that we are able to find new ways of moving forward, and it is therefore important that we are aware of the many ways in which we can find solutions.

People process information in many different ways. It starts with touching, perceiving what is around us as well as what is inside us: tuning in. We then put all the things that we perceive into words; into pictures; into sculptures and music; into butterflies in our stomachs; into actions. Most therapies, and also most teaching methods, only emphasise one or two of these modes of processing. The activities in this book are aimed at using all of the different modes to help children open up new ways of finding solutions. We also find that a significant number of the children with whom we work have problems associated with being in contact and we actively set out to get these children in contact with themselves, with the other children and with us; to be in touch.

In summary, our approach to groupwork draws on a combination of behavioural and cognitive psychology, humanistic therapy, psychodynamics, group dynamics, creative groupwork and transpersonal psychology.

Our central aims are to help the children to have:

- more understanding of their own behaviour;
- more control over their behaviour;
- more positive self-esteem;
- more positive social relationships.

CHAPTER 2

The Role of the Therapist

We started the process of developing our groupwork by looking at our own experiences, both as children as well as within our teaching and therapist-roles.

If we look back on our experiences as children, both at home and at school, we can probably all remember times when our confidence in ourselves was rocked by something our parents or a teacher said or did and, conversely, times when we received praise or rewards which made us feel better about ourselves. One of the authors can remember her father trying to explain long division to her and becoming quite angry when she did not grasp it immediately. Of course, there was no hope for her from then onwards and she developed the idea that she could not do long division. On the other hand, a teacher telling her that he loved to hear her read Shakespeare was a great boost to her confidence and also made her feel much more positive about the difficult language of Shakespeare.

We take the view that the children in the groups that we run are more likely to learn new behaviours if the adults notice their positive behaviour. By the time the children come to us, their parents and teachers are at their wits end and the children are used to hearing a great deal about their negative behaviour. So, the direct feedback which we give to the children is always positive.

We also recognise that people learn more from each other than from teachers or therapists. Moreover, if we are able to facilitate this 'learning from each other' process by creating the right positive environment and making the children aware of their own choices, it will help them to continue to use this process positively after the group has ended.

The choice of working with groups was based on our work with children individually. We had so much fun on our own with the children, that we felt we could do it for years on end. The children's self-esteem increased, and they started to think more logically and found their unacceptable feelings and stories were accepted by a grown-up. There was just one problem; they never acted out. We never saw the behaviour for which the children had been referred, and we were not sure whether we were making changes in that area. So we decided to put all of the children together in one group. We got what we had wanted. After four sessions with our first group we felt that we were ending up being policemen and not therapists. After a short honeymoon the children started kicking each other and launched territorial wars over and by means of coffee-tables, chairs and pencils. We found ourselves sitting on the arms of their chairs, either to control them or to protect them. We were becoming more anxious with every moment that passed, with every move they made, every look they gave. Do you recognise the pattern?

Patterns of Anxiety & Control

> The inner pattern of anxiety leads to over-control.
> The outer pattern of over-control leads to imbalance, to acting out.

We sensed that increasing control or speeding-up the activity programme would not be the solution. We decided to consult everyone possible and following this we introduced two helpful changes:

1 Wrestling

We introduced wrestling. A golden rule: *quite often the best solution is 'more of the same'.* If the children wanted to compete, to establish a pecking order, they would get the chance. It would also help them to learn about rules – 'to compete but not to hurt' and about boundaries – 'there is a time for everything'. It worked well for that particular group and we were surprised by how much they respected each other in the wrestling. We still use it, although not as standard practice, just when we feel it is needed.

2 Reflective Guidance

The more crucial of the two changes, which we still use and keep refining, could be called 'reflective guidance'. Whenever we finished the therapy session, we were always full of comments about all the things we had observed and experienced. We had to 'let off steam' and make sense for ourselves of all that had happened. Somebody suggested that we should not wait until we had left the room, but that we should do it continually during the session, in front of the children.

We started to talk to each other about the children, in their presence. If they behaved in a negative way, we refrained from approaching them directly with 'don't do it, don't even try to ...' Instead, we would explore the behaviour together, trying to translate – tentatively – the message it conveyed and suggesting the different ways in which it could be dealt with more constructively; if possible by using as an example previous instances when the child had done well. We have found that this actually encourages the child who is being talked about to listen, because they are not being put on the spot or singled out in the way that could often happen at home or at school. In such situations the only option for the child can be to close the shutters and not take in what is being said. Discussing the behaviour also provides a model of two adults, working together in a calm and reasonable way, who are not provoked into anger by the behaviour. An example of such an interaction might be as follows:

The child, John, is constantly talking nonsense or making funny noises and not respecting when others speak.

JD It seems that John is having difficulty listening at the moment.
SB Yes, it is difficult to continue with the group activity, isn't it?
JD I wonder if he wants everybody's attention. Perhaps he could wait until the break. He made some good jokes at break-time last week.

We also occasionally make positive comments in this manner, particularly about the group as a whole, for example, 'I really liked the way the group listened so well to the story just now'.

There are a number of important ingredients that are woven into this style of guidance, which can be summarised as follows:

REFLECTIVE GUIDANCE

- We invite the children to control themselves and leave the initiative with them. We acknowledge that when they find their way out of a hole they have been digging for themselves. This will enhance their self-control and their self-respect. The word 'honour' springs to mind. We try to solve conflicts in ways which mean that nobody loses face.
- We positively reframe negative behaviour as an attempt to convey a message or a need.
- We will not ignore negative behaviour.

- We state that a person has a choice about how to communicate messages and some methods might be more successful than others. It is thus worthwhile to think before you act.
- We try – tentatively once again, as it is not interpretation – to give words to their messages. A child keeps knocking or kicking on the door until you open it. Therefore we must actively listen and make the children aware that we are listening.
- We try to make sense of children's confusion and offer alternative stories or discourses for their experiences and their behaviour.
- We also help them to find words to describe their experiences and hope that they can begin to use language when it is more effective to do so.
- We provide a role model of non-paranoid thinking. 'What you are doing isn't seen as a threat to me; so there is no need for me to defend myself; we can start to listen to each other.'
- We also provide an adult model that differs from what they are used to; we work together in a calm and reasonable way.

Things don't have to be as they are.
You can make a difference!

Working in this way is extremely challenging and not as easy as we have made it sound. When perhaps six children – all of whom have been driving parents and/or teachers to distraction – are gathered together, the result can be explosive. It takes considerable patience and trust in each other to work in this way. We have had to reduce our own needs for control in order for the children to find a locus of control within themselves. We have learned that this process can bring about change and this has helped us to trust the process and let things happen. There can be confusion and anxiety in the midst of the mayhem and for this reason it has been helpful at times to have observers tell us about things that we have not been able to see because we have been too involved. They can also sometimes pick up ways in which individuals are showing the first signs of change before we notice them; we can then look at, reinforce and build upon these changes.

We have noticed that the groups have brought about changes in us. Remaining calm within such a setting has enabled us to remain calm within other settings that might previously have caused us to become short-tempered or anxious, for example with our colleagues or our own children.

Every situation, every group is a new experience. It is important to stay focused in your approach as a therapist or a teacher, namely to:

- Respect the children at all times.
- Help them to make sense of the situation.
- Invite them to join in positive, shared control over the situation.

CHAPTER 3

Setting Up the Group

Structure

The groupwork programme runs for a total of ten weekly sessions, each lasting 60 minutes for the younger groups and 75 minutes for the older groups. As the groups run during school time, we also have a half-term break in the programme.

When we started to run our groups we planned every single minute of the sessions and were anxious in case we had not planned enough. We had come across articles about groupwork for children which advised the therapist to have more than one room and have activities laid out in these different rooms, in order for everything to run smoothly.

We soon moved away from that concept. The main reason being that most of the children were especially disruptive at school in uncontrolled activities, for example in the playground. Therefore we started to ease up and slow down our sessions. This allowed more free space for spontaneity and acting out. It also gave more opportunities for us to talk in a reflective way, because it did not matter whether the activities were completed. It gave the children more responsibility for getting on with the programme and not getting bored. It also allowed for more improvisation. If children want to act out a certain story to experience it more truly, they can adapt the programme accordingly. If they want to discuss anything, there is time to discuss it.

Each session now loosely follows a basic structure:

Start: What we will do today.
News: Each child gets a chance to discuss something about their week.
Positive feedback: We tell each of the children what we have especially noticed or appreciated during the previous week and sometimes also give them a task for the forthcoming remainder of the session.
Breathing: An exercise in self-control.
Activity
Break: 5 to 10 minutes (drink and biscuit).
Trust game
Story or activity
End: What was today about?
Countdown: Everybody is sitting down and we count from ten to one in order to calm down together before the children are allowed to leave the room.

The structure is an important way of providing predictability and security, and we remind the children of this at the start of each session.

As we have already indicated, we give each child frequent feedback about their behaviour. Before the children start in the group we hold meetings with them and their parent(s) or carer and identify three individual target areas in which the child and the parents hope to see improvements. With these targets in mind, we will give each child entirely positive feedback about their progress at the beginning of each session. During the session we also give the children feedback about their behaviour and the effect that it is having on others. At the end of the ten-session programme each child is given a certificate of attendance, outlining the areas in which we feel the child has made most progress, particularly in relation to their targets.

You will note that the sessions for the younger age groups are more highly structured and that we give the feedback on a particular session directly at the end of that session, rather than at the beginning of the next one.

We feel that the use of metaphors and stories is very helpful in therapy. It is not necessary to tell somebody what to do or to tell them off. Instead, you can tell them about similar problems and possible solutions, with a free choice as to what to take on board, encouraging learning in a way which respects their integrity.

Furthermore, the person will form a picture, an image or even an inner film of the story. It is easier to remember in this way as it has more aspects. The image becomes a stage on which you can try out variations of the story, problem or variations of your feelings. Inner drama therapy or inner exposure in vitro, call it what you will.

With this in mind, the central activity over the ten sessions for the older groups is the reading of a story, *Bubble Gum Guy* (Drost, 1997), in five chapters throughout the life of the group. This story emphasises one of the main themes of the group, namely self-control. It is the story of a child who has bubble gum irremovably fixed in his mouth, which bursts over himself and others when he gets angry. Through the help of a pearl-diver, he learns to control his breathing and express himself more positively (for a fuller description of the story, see the Appendix).

The breathing exercise mentioned above in the outline of the session structure is linked to this story: each week, the children hold their breath and try to improve on how long they can hold it from the previous week. By doing so, the children will learn to control themselves and to develop the ability to wait. They also gain self-esteem from the exercise. The other thought behind this weekly exercise is one of anchoring! The children usually start to practise at home and in this way they will take the therapy home.

It is hoped that all of the experiences in the group will be anchored to this breathing exercise and might be brought back to memory or even life long after the group has finished.

For the younger groups we use a tree as a central symbol around which to organise the activities and to anchor the group in their everyday world.

Over the course of the group the children receive several worksheets. In the first week we give them their personal folder to keep their work in. Often the children will decorate the folders, while they are listening to the story and/or during breaktimes. They take their folder home at the end of the ten-session programme.

Themes

All our activities are designed to support work around various themes:

Getting to know each other/Breaking the ice
Listening to each other
Empathy
Trust
Choices
Problem-solving

Self-identity and Self-esteem
Expression of feelings and opinions
Working together
Endings

As explained above the activities are also designed to address as many different aspects of these themes as possible. If we talk about listening, we challenge the children to listen to not only words but to non-verbal language and to emotions. We try to use every possible channel of internal information processing including words, reason, poetry, acting, drama, drawing, clay-modelling, guided imagery and silence. If we get stuck in life, it is important that we are able to find new ways out; therefore it is important to be aware of the many ways solutions can be found.

While each group is presented with the same material, we do not necessarily keep the activities in the same order. We have to remain flexible because groups vary considerably; for example, one group took much longer to settle and start working cooperatively, so we had to delay the reading of the story and concentrate instead on trying to build a group feeling. After each session the therapists have one hour together to formulate feedback and to discuss what would be appropriate for the next session, given the needs of particular individuals, and what has happened in the previous session.

We have chosen the themes listed above with care. The group meets over quite a short period of time and therefore it is important that we facilitate the children getting to know each other fairly quickly. Most of the children have problems with peer relationships and many have short attention spans, so we place emphasis on listening to each other and empathy. Many children get into trouble because of their belief systems, eg, that the only way to deal with conflict is to hit out, so we challenge these belief systems and ask the children to think about other ways of resolving conflict.

It may seem strange to stress endings, but we do so for two reasons. Although the group meets over a short period, the feeling of being part of the group is strong, and this is important if the experience is to have any effect; therefore it is important that we pay attention to the ending of the sessions and acknowledge the feelings about this. Secondly, many of the children have experienced significant losses – usually of fathers from the home – and we feel it is important to help them to express some of their feelings of loss and also to look at ways of helping them come to terms with that loss and any future loss.

We aim to evaluate progress through pre- and post-treatment questionnaires to parents and schools. These are simple rating scales: those for parents are based on the agreed aims for the child; those sent to schools are more generalised (see Appendix).

CHAPTER 4

Embedding the Group in its Context

In this section we examine the type of children we take into our groups in the Child & Family Consultation Service. We conclude by looking at how these types of groups or any of the exercises can be transferred to other settings.

Within a therapeutic setting children often arrive after many other things have been tried. The children already seem to be stuck in a corner, and labelled, showing certain defensive behaviours (which strangely enough are mostly perceived by adults as attacks). The children are either referred to our service with the label 'disruptive and aggressive behaviour' or 'depressive and compulsive behaviour'. Regardless of the label, the adults around the children are desperate and do not know what to do or how to achieve control.

Another group of children referred to our service are the victims of bullying, on the basis that if a child is bullied there must be something wrong with them as a person. It is not surprising that blaming the victim for being bullied leads to more depression and low self-esteem. Blaming the victim, or even the bully, is in itself an escape from admitting that we, as adults, do not know what to do or how to control the situation.

We initially set out by putting all the aggressive, disruptive children in one group; these were mostly children who had been excluded from school on several occasions. Once, we had the opportunity to run two groups simultaneously and we divided them into a group of 'toughies' and a group of 'softies'. To our surprise, we could not tell the difference. If anything, the toughies were far more sociable and more in control of themselves, but that might have been due to the fact that they were fewer in number. It was clear that the softies had their own ways of irritating and being mean to each other.

The question is 'do toughies and softies exist?' We are all aware of people who get into trouble because they are more sensitive than others. Modern-day Robin Hoods who dig tunnels and fight the police because they love trees, because they want to prevent us from destroying our planet. Or the child who loses his temper because he is wrongly accused of something. Unfortunately, even if there is not a reason for being cross with the child in the first place, once he loses his temper everyone has a reason to be cross with them. A no-win situation. Could it be that toughies are just strong at the broken places?

Once you begin to think about selecting children, first think about the above questions, and start to remove the labels the children have already been given. We are now of the opinion that our groups are suitable for a wide variety of children, but we still assess these children before they come into the group – not just to get to know them but also to remove the labels.

It is important that the group is not seen as a remedy, the be all and end all, the answer to everything. We try to examine whether the right things are in place in the child's environment for the child to make proper use of the group. It is no use helping a child to get out of a corner if the whole world keeps putting him back in that corner. For example, in some families increased self-esteem and assertiveness in a child will be perceived as a further threat to the parents, who are unable to let go of their negative battle with the child. In such cases we prefer to address the family issues first. Another example is the child who is being bullied or is part of a bullying ring at school. Here, we feel it necessary first to address the bullying issue with the school.

We will also look into the history of the child. If things have been very difficult from birth onwards, there might well be some learning difficulties or other organic difficulties that could contribute to the child's difficult behaviour. If things have previously always been fine and have a sudden onset, we would be curious as to whether we could find any organic or environmental causes for the change. Abnormal and persistent behaviour in children is often an attempt to get a message across. They do not feel in control, and this is sometimes because they have literally been abused.

To summarise, we assess children because we want to rule out certain causal factors which might need to be addressed differently.

> *Although children might benefit from the group, the group cannot be a substitute for primary needs, such as child protection, medical needs, good parenting and good education.*

This means that good communication with everybody concerned with the child is just as important as the group. Even if the child is able to make good use of the group and there are no other major problems, it is essential that the people around the child are able to adapt to the changes in that child and are able to adopt some of our basic views about the child. For that purpose we will see the parent(s) or carer before and after the group and, if necessary, more often. We also give written feedback about the group to the child's school. Ideally, we would like to run parallel groups for parents and would like to involve teachers in running these groups, or the activities, in a different format in the schools.

If we were to talk about transferring these experiences to different settings, it is not so much the whole group programme we would like to transfer, but the basic underlying approaches. The main aims of the group are:

- To create a safe, healthy environment in which children can explore and develop;
- To accept all feelings and thoughts, although not necessarily all actions;
- To help the children to find different, acceptable ways to act, by opening up different channels through the variety of activities;
- Not to force children, but to let them be in control of their own progress.

You do not need a therapeutic setting such as a Child & Family Consultation Service to help children in this way. Neither do you need to wait until the children are having major behavioural and emotional problems. Children will probably be more able to benefit from and contribute to this type of groupwork if it is offered before they feel that they have become stuck in a corner.

A couple of schools have already used our group format to run their own groups, and the results have been very encouraging. The children appear to be well able to appreciate and respect the difference between the group and their normal lessons. Most importantly, the group seemed to allow children to get away from the labels that had been given to them by the school, eg, a notoriously difficult child was shown to be very caring and responsible. Good communication between the group leaders and the teachers will help the children to generalise the things they learn in the group into the class setting.

When selecting children for a group in a school, it is important not to put all the most difficult children into one group. Actually, the greater the variety in skills and characters, the more the children will be able to learn from one another. Other issues to take into consideration when setting up a group in a school are clearly allocated time and space.

We have not experienced confidentiality as an issue, even if two or three children are from the same class. As mentioned above, the nature of the group is not one of uprooting one's deepest secrets and feelings, as 'therapy' is often misunderstood. It is about how the children relate to each other in the present. It is not the confidentiality as such that is crucial, but the boundaries around the group: what happens in the group is dealt with in the group, in the positive, reflective way that we have described. This unconditional, positive environment could be undermined if there were negative consequences outside the group. The same, of course could be said for the boundaries around a positive school environment.

When running a group in a school or in a clinic, it is important to remember what it is all about: we are trying to make a difference, not to create a band of angels. We do not expect children to stop being angry. As the result of the group process we would like people, whether they are children, parents or teachers:

- To feel all right about themselves.
- To know that despite everything they have been through, despite everything they may have been accused of, they are people in their own right and have their own wisdom to use.
- To know that they have a choice in every situation of how to react and how to behave.
- To have a richness of ways in which they can find solutions for themselves.
- To respect themselves.
- To respect others.
- To feel in control of themselves.
- To feel they are able to influence the world around them.
- To feel that they have unique gifts to give to the world.

Part I

CHAPTER 5

Theoretical Background

When we first discussed setting up groups, or when we encountered difficulties and wanted to refer to other therapists' theoretical background and experiences, we turned to the literature. We have found very little specifically relating to primary-school aged children. In a chapter entitled 'Historical Development of Group Psychotherapy', in a book on groupwork with children and adolescents, edited by Dwivedi (1993), Patrick McGrath refers to four sources who describe work with adolescents and only one who describes work with children, Samuel Slavson (1979). Currently there is more groupwork going on with children in various settings, using a variety of methods and approaches, but it seems that there is little which is based, as is our approach, on humanistic psychology and psychotherapy.

Group therapy with adults is well established and has been most heavily influenced by psychoanalytical theory although, in the very early stages in the United States, it seems that the techniques were more didactic than therapeutic. Trigant Burrow, an American psychiatrist, is credited with running the first psychoanalytic groups although without the approval of Freud whom he had met in Europe and believed that he was following. Other psychiatrists and psychoanalysts followed, including Foulkes (1975), who was instrumental in the setting up of therapeutic communities, and Lewin (1952), who was the first person to use the phrase 'group dynamics'. All of them saw the individual as both operating within, and influenced by, the social group which is more than the sum of its parts. The therapeutic group, with a group leader, offers an opportunity for change and healing by giving participants the opportunity to act out and work through their difficulties in relating to others.

One of the most influential theorists in the adult field was Wilfred Bion (1962), a psychoanalyst who worked alongside Foulkes with soldiers suffering from 'military neurosis' arising out of their experiences in the Second World War. This phenomenon, which was called 'shell-shock' in the First World War, we would now call post-traumatic stress disorder. Out of this work, Bion developed theories to explain why some groups of people do not achieve their goals. He proposed that this happened because the members of the group shared certain unconscious basic assumptions that prevented a task from being completed. According to him, there were three types of basic assumptions that a group could have: either that the group leader will magically bring about solutions without the participants having to do anything; or they share a belief that two members of the group are going to pair up and produce a new leader who will find solutions; or that they will either have to fight or run away from some external threat as the only means of self-preservation. In contrast to this type of group, which gets nowhere, there exists the work group whose members are aware of the need to learn and develop their skills and to contribute fully to the group. This type of group is able to grow and develop. Bion sees the task of the group leader as helping the group to work through these three basic assumptions and take responsibility for their own lives. In the groups which we run, we see a manifestation of all these basic assumptions at one time or another and, as the group members are children and we are adults, particularly the first assumption, which pushes us, as group leaders, to take control. We are always working towards the children taking responsibility for their own behaviour.

Yalom (1970) attempted to analyse the complex process of therapeutic change in groups and outlined eleven curative factors that he felt described how people improve in group therapy. To summarise:

- First, he felt that those joining a group would encounter people who had improved and they would therefore be given hope.
- They would also realise that their problems were universal, part of the human condition, and not unique to them.
- There is also a certain amount of learning about group process, which is implicit rather than explicit, and can be generalised in the outside world.
- Clients in a group can receive through giving and helping others in the group.
- They can recreate their own primary families in the group and, through reality testing, exploration and testing out, find new ways of behaving with others which are less influenced by primary relationships.
- Members of a group will develop their social skills.
- They will learn through imitation or modelling themselves on the therapist.
- They will learn about how they relate to others and how others relate to them.
- They become part of a group which has a life and identity of its own and which is cohesive.
- They may have the opportunity for catharsis, for experiencing strong feelings that have previously been contained, in a safely held environment.
- Lastly, there is the experience of being deeply involved in a group of people struggling with the same issues of existence.

We recognise all the possibilities that Yalom delineates in our groups except perhaps for the first, which applies more to long-term, open groups than our short-term, closed groups where everyone starts together. The feedback that we give the children at the end of the courses, on their certificates, should reflect some of these curative factors. We are also mindful that children are referred to our service by other people; they do not refer themselves, so although they cannot be forced to attend our groups, and a few children have 'voted with their feet', they do not have the same level of choice to attend as would an adult.

Samuel Slavson (1979), perhaps because of his background as a school teacher, was a pioneer in bringing a psychoanalytic approach to working with groups of children. He called his work Activity Group Therapy, and it was based on a permissive and accepting approach that allowed children to take their conflicts into the group so that they could be observed and worked with. He believed, as do we, that every individual has creative potential and can be helped to become a constructive member of a group through the need for contact, even if this has become distorted. He did not work with children through verbal interpretation but described what he did as 'an ego-level form of therapy'. He differentiated this work from psychoanalytical groupwork with adults, where the individual becomes the centre of attention in the group from time to time. With children, the group itself is the therapy.

Although there are differences in the way Slavson worked and the way we set up our groups, there are many similarities. Slavson operated within more physical space than we do, with a choice of activities, which children could move between. We work in one room and have a set programme of activities planned for each session but this is used with flexibility. Slavson saw the therapist as less involved than we do. For him, the therapist functioned in the psychoanalytical mode of the 'blank screen' on to which the child could project. Our main aim is the same, although we also wish to strengthen the autonomous potential in children. We also share the hope of modelling good parenting although Slavson, again, describes this in more psychoanalytical terms than we do. He also talks about 'unconditional acceptance' by the therapist, a function which echoes one of the requirements of a good therapist in the humanistic model that was developed particularly by Carl Rogers (1961). Dwivedi (1993) describes the disillusionment with taking Slavson's approach in totality because of the 'lightning spread' of acting-out behaviours that can make a therapeutic approach irrelevant. This has been our experience too, and has led us to being more proactive in our choice of children for the groups. The group should not become overwhelmed by the behaviour of the children to such an extent that a feeling of danger develops.

Another approach that has been used in groupwork with children is that of Cognitive & Behavioural Therapy, that uses the group as part of the process of reinforcement of good behaviour. The approach tends to be highly structured and based around problem-solving and learning new skills, for example, social skills or assertiveness skills. There may also be attempts to alter faulty cognitions that may be leading the individual into difficulty and may involve using the group for roleplay, modelling, etc. Behavioural approaches can be used in groups to deal with very specific problems such as soiling. We use elements of these approaches in our groups; for example, the *Situations* activity is designed to help children confront their faulty perceptions and consider alternatives. Our use of positive feedback is designed to reinforce appropriate behaviour and divert attention from the inappropriate.

More specific tools and techniques for groupwork with children are described by Dwivedi (1993) and include play, activities, exercises and games, art therapy, relaxation, visualisation and drama, all of which we use in our groups to encourage children to express aspects of themselves that they may be unable or unwilling to reveal in other contexts.

It seems that our approach to working with children in groups has taken elements from many of the different models that have been developed over the last century, that use the group experience to improve social functioning and relating. What they all seem to have in common is something related to releasing human potential and creativity – the core of our work.

PART II ACTIVITIES

Part II

Groups for 5 to 7 year olds

Although we originally started to work with older age groups, children aged from eight to eleven, we soon extended our groupwork to younger children, because we experienced an increase in referrals to the Child & Family Consultation Service, both for reasons of uncontrollable, acting-out behaviour, as well as for reasons of low self-esteem and self-confidence. One would hope that working with the younger age group means an earlier point of intervention and more chance of making a difference. Teachers and other professionals who work with children have noted that young children seem less and less prepared for school life. Some children seem to have grown up relating only to televisions and computers, rather than having learned about social relationships. How will they manage in a school full of other children and adults? The longer that we ran these groups, the more it became clear to us that they were about helping the children to be able to relate to others, to be part of multiple relationships simultaneously, to be part of groups.

Working with the children aged from five to seven, one has to take into account that they have a short concentration span and thus any activities have to be shorter and more active. One cannot depend on their reading and writing skills. The activities need to be less verbal and must use other, more concrete ways to reach the children, such as visual cues and choices, tangible objects and movement games. Of course, older children with learning difficulties require a similar approach. Each session is slightly shorter than for the older children, (those aged eight to eleven), lasting for one hour instead of one and a quarter hours.

With younger children it is even more important to make the structure of the group predictable. This will help them to feel safe and contained. Therefore we have developed little traditions and leading themes to provide continuity over the sessions.

One of the themes used is that of the tree. We have tried to create activities around the tree as a symbol. To us, the tree is a symbol of growth and strength. The tree needs to develop its roots, its foundation, as well as its branches and leaves. We start every session with a short poem and go through the movements of waking up in the hollow of a tree and climbing down to enter the group. At the end of the session each of us climbs up our tree again (see *Climbing down the tree*). Other activities can also be connected to the tree in simple ways. For example, if the children have to draw something about themselves, like their favourite animal, they do it on leaf-shaped pieces of paper that can be stuck on a big tree on the wall. We also encourage the children to observe and draw trees and to find their own favourite tree in their environment.

The symbol of the tree is used to anchor the meaning of the group in a symbol that the children come across almost every day, hopefully for years to come. After the group sessions have ended, trees will never be the same again and will always carry a special meaning for the children.

Of course, it is possible to choose another central symbol for your group. In an inner city, where trees are hard to find, one might want to use birds, clouds or even building bricks as symbols. One of our groups, all fostered children in temporary placements, used the theme of making a journey on a sailing boat, to reflect the transient situation they were in. After all, they had been uprooted, often many times, and could not even count on the trees in their life to stay around.

We also introduced the use of puppets in the infants group. Step-by-step, session-by-session, the puppets develop. Starting as simple socks the puppets must learn to listen and to see, before they can have a mouth and learn to speak.

It is incredible how honest puppets can be – even on the hand of an adult – and how easily children can express themselves through the puppets. Puppets are often allowed to lose control and act out, where the person manipulating the puppet might restrain themselves. Strangely enough, it also works the other way around, whereby the puppets of uncontrolled children can be quite sensible and insightful as to what is happening in the group.

Groupwork with younger children is very rewarding. They are keen to take part in the activities and keen to learn. They are often more physical in their approach, which means cuddles as well as lashing out.

Groups for 8 to 11 year olds

Part II

The activities for the older children are built along the same themes as the activities for the younger groups. Instead of using the symbol of the tree as a thread through the sessions, we use the story of Bubble Gum Guy, which was especially written for these groups. The breathing activity that is repeated every session is linked with the story. It gives the children a chance to practice at home, and years later they may still think about the group if they try to hold their breath under water.

Some of the activities for these groups are more complicated and require better reading skills. However, there are also some quite simple activities that are used for the younger age groups as well. We have noticed that the older children sometimes like to regress and play games such as *The Den*. At times, where a group finds it difficult to jell even after five or six sessions, we have found it useful to fall back on the activities that were designed for the younger age group.

In the older age group there are often more opportunities for discussions. It still should be emphasised that it is not important to have lengthy discussions, or to 'therapise' what has been raised. It is important to accept, acknowledge and to then get on with the activities.

We have noticed that there can be a danger of over-emphasising 'opening up' or 'talking about feelings'. This can result in a competitiveness amongst the children as to who has been the most sad and unlucky. When these groups come to an end the children may relapse into depression or acting out behaviour, as it was consistently rewarded with attention and safety in the group.

Part II

Planning a ten-session programme

It is difficult to list the following activities either according to age, when they occur in the programme or the themes that they address. Various activities are suitable for both age ranges. Some activities are especially designed for the early phase of the course while other activities can be used throughout the course. Every activity addresses multiple themes.

There is a basic structure to the development of the sessions. Each group will start with activities to allow the children to get to know each other and to build up trust. Early in the group programme we focus on listening activities and turn taking. We then introduce activities that require empathy and trying to understand other people. Next, we will move to activities in which the children can explore and express their own feelings and opinions. From there we move on to exploring social situations and problem-solving; finally we focus on losses and endings.

Each group is different. Some groups find it difficult to sit still and require lots of dynamic activities. Other groups like to chat and talk and are really stimulated by the more verbal activities. Some groups find it easier to start with whole group trust activities while other groups feel safer to start with paired working.

Flexibility is essential. You need to be able to adapt the programme to the needs of your particular group. Following are two examples of a ten-session programme for each age group. You will note that some activities stay the same over the examples as they are part of the basic structure.

5 TO 7 YEAR OLDS: SAMPLE TEN-SESSION PROGRAMME

Session 1

- Introduction and Rules
- Climbing Down the Tree
- Name Game, the web
- Binary Choices
- *Break*
- Draw a Tree
- Be a tree
- Feedback with puppets
- Climbing Up the Tree

Session 2

- Climbing Down the Tree
- News
- Name Game with cuddly toy
- Funny Walks
- Chinese Whispers with drawings
- *Break*
- Chinese Whispers with words
- Introduction of puppets
- Individualise puppets
- Feedback with puppets
- Climbing Up the Tree

Session 3

- Climbing Down the Tree
- News
- Opposite Sides of the Room
- *Break*
- Snuggles and Grizzles
- Feedback with puppets
- Climbing Up the Tree

Session 4

- Climbing Down the Tree
- News
- Families
- Put eyes on the puppets
- Sad Tears, Happy Tears
- *Break*
- Favourite Animal
- Play 'I-spy' with puppets
- Feedback with puppets
- Climbing Up the Tree

Session 5

- Climbing Down the Tree
- News
- Labyrinth
- *Break*
- What's my Line?
- Feedback with puppets
- Find your own tree during the half-term break
- Climbing Up the Tree

Session 6

- Climbing Down the Tree
- News and talk about the trees they found
- Statues
- *Break*
- Put mouths on the puppets
- What haven't you been able to say?
- Feedback with puppets
- Climbing Up the Tree

Session 7

- Climbing Down the Tree
- News
- Play puppet scenes
- *Break:* Campfire
- Circle
- Feedback with puppets
- Climbing Up the Tree

Session 8

- Climbing Down the Tree
- News
- Losses
- *Break*
- Continue Losses
- Be a Tree
- Feedback with puppets
- Climbing Up the Tree

Session 9

- Climbing Down the Tree
- News
- Opposite Sides of the Room
- *Break*
- The Group Tree
- Ten Ways to Walk the Room
- Feedback with puppets
- Climbing Up the Tree

Session 10

- Climb Down the Tree
- News
- Games that the children propose: Simon says, Grandmother's footsteps, Sticky fingers, The sun shines on, etc.
- *Break*
- Funny Walks
- Certificates
- Climbing Up the Tree

5 TO 7 YEAR OLDS: SAMPLE TEN-SESSION PROGRAMME

Session 1

- Introduction and rules
- Climbing Down the Tree
- Name Game, the web
- Opposite sides of the room
- *Break*
- Draw a Tree
- Be a Tree
- Feedback with puppets
- Climbing Up the Tree

Session 2

- Climbing Down the Tree
- News
- Name Game with cuddly toy
- Mirroring
- Empathy Riddles
- *Break*
- Favourite Animal
- Introduction of puppets
- Individualise puppets
- Feedback with puppets
- Climbing Up the Tree

Session 3

- Climbing Down the Tree
- News
- Families
- *Break*
- Labyrinth
- Feedback with puppets
- Climbing Up the Tree

Session 4

- Climbing Down the Tree
- News
- What's my Line?
- Put eyes on the puppets
- Sad Tears, Happy Tears
- *Break*
- Funny Walks
- Play 'I-spy' with puppets
- Feedback with puppets
- Climbing Up the Tree

Session 5

- Climbing Down the Tree
- News
- Boxes and Bellies
- *Break*

- What Happens Next?
- Feedback with puppets
- Find your own tree during the half-term break
- Climbing Up the Tree

Session 6

- Climbing Down the Tree
- News and talk about the trees they found
- Ten Ways to Walk the Room
- *Break*
- The Den
- Put mouths on the puppets
- What haven't you been able to say?
- Feedback with puppets
- Climbing Up the Tree

Session 7

- Climbing Down the Tree
- News
- Magic Box
- *Break:* Campfire
- Volcano
- Four Corners of the Room
- Feedback with puppets
- Climbing Up the Tree

Session 8

- Climbing Down the Tree
- News
- The Den
- *Break*
- The Group Tree
- Snuggles and Grizzles
- Feedback with puppets
- Climbing Up the Tree

Session 9

- Climbing Down the Tree
- News
- Losses
- *Break*
- Continue Losses
- Be a Tree
- Feedback with puppets
- Climbing Up the Tree

Session 10

- Climbing Down the Tree
- News
- Empathy Riddles
- *Break*
- End Game
- Certificates
- Climbing Up the Tree

Ages 8 to 11

8 TO 11 YEAR OLDS: SAMPLE TEN-SESSION PROGRAMME

Session 1

- Introduction and rules
- Name Game
- Bubble Gum Guy, part one
- Breathing
- *Break*
- How do you do?
- Ending: What was today about?

Session 2

- Feedback and news
- Breathing
- Mirroring
- What's my Line?
- *Break*
- Operation Abandon ship
- Ending: What was today about?

Session 3

- Feedback and news
- Breathing
- Families
- *Break*
- Situations (role-play)
- Bubble Gum Guy, part two
- Ending: What was today about?

Session 4

- Feedback and news
- Breathing
- Rap and Right
- *Break*
- Volcano
- Continue: Rap and Right
- Ending: What was today about?

Session 5

- Feedback and news
- Breathing
- Labyrinth
- Guided fantasy: The Horse
- *Break*
- Bubble Gum Guy, part three
- Rescue Operation
- Ending: What was today about?

Session 6

- Feedback and news
- Breathing
- Empathy Riddles
- *Break*
- Circle
- Sentence Completion
- Ending: What was today about?

Session 7

- Feedback and news
- Breathing
- Bubble Gum Guy, part four
- *Break:* Campfire
- What Happens Next?
- Ending: What was today about?

Session 8

- Feedback and news
- Breathing
- Guided fantasy 2222!
- *Break:* Campfire or alternative activity
- Four Corners of the Room.
- Ending: What was today about?

Session 9

- Feedback and news
- Breathing
- Losses
- *Break*
- Robbery
- Ending: What was today about?

Session 10

- News
- Breathing
- End Game
- *Break*
- Bubble Gum Guy, part five
- Feedback Certificates & pebble
- Ending and goodbyes

8 TO 11 YEAR OLDS: SAMPLE TEN-SESSION PROGRAMME

Session 1

- Introduction and rules
- Name Game, the web
- Bubble Gum Guy, part one
- Breathing
- *Break*
- Sentence Completion
- Funny Walks
- Ending: What was today about?

Session 2

- Feedback and news
- Breathing
- Families
- *Break*
- Boxes and Bellies
- Ending: What was today about?

Session 3

- Feedback and news
- Breathing
- What's my Line
- *Break*
- Bubble Gum Guy, part two
- Magic Box
- Ending: What was today about?

Session 4

- Feedback and news
- Breathing
- Judge too Much!
- *Break*
- Labyrinth
- Empathy Riddles
- Ending: What was today about?

Session 5

- Feedback and news
- Breathing
- Bubble Gum Guy, part three
- *Break*
- Rescue Operation
- Empathy Riddles
- Ending: What was today about?

Session 6

- Feedback and news
- Breathing
- Four Corners of the Room
- *Break*
- What Happens Next?
- Ending: What was today about?

Session 7

- Feedback and news
- Breathing
- Bubble Gum Guy, part four
- *Break*: Campfire
- Guided fantasy: The Horse
- Ending: What was today about?

Session 8

- Feedback and news
- Breathing
- Operation Op!
- *Break*
- Mirroring
- Situations
- Ending: What was today about?

Session 9

- Feedback and news
- Breathing
- Losses
- *Break*
- Losses continued
- Circle
- Ending: What was today about?

Session 10

- News
- Breathing
- End Game
- *Break*
- Bubble Gum Guy, part five
- Feedback Certificates & pebble
- Ending and goodbyes

The Activities

The activities on the following pages are listed firstly according to age, starting with the activities for the younger age group, followed by activities that can be used by both age groups and finally those activities which are solely for the older age group. The general Introduction is placed at the head of the activities.

To facilitate picking and mixing the activities into a ten-session programme, each description also indicates which themes are addressed and which other activities can be used as alternatives or as follow ups.

When you evaluate the previous session it is helpful to formulate goals for the following session. Do you want to work on listening, empathy, expression, problem-solving? Do you need activities that do not require a lot of verbal skills? Do you want to encourage paired and group working? These questions will lead you to the themes, through which you can find the appropriate activities. An alphabetical list of the activities and the related themes can be found in Appendix 4.

Session advice: 1-2

Themes:
ICE-BREAKER
LISTENING

Introduction

Aim **To welcome the children, tell them what the group is about and talk about the rules.**

Welcome everybody to this first group session.

Today is the first of ten weeks that we will be together.

We will start with a short introduction, to tell you what this group is about. Then we will talk about the rules of the group and what we will do today.

All of you have come here because you have experienced difficulties at home or at school, with peers, teachers or parents.

Some of you might have been blamed for these difficulties; you may also feel more like the victim.

This group is first of all about being yourself and about having a good time. People might tell you that you are always getting into trouble, that you are always shouting or always crying. People might call you names.

We will invite you to discover yourself in a positive way.

We will have games, questions, stories, all kind of activities to do.

Most importantly, we want to help you to make your own decisions, about how you want to be, what you want to achieve, what is important for you.

We also want you to look at the best ways of achieving your goals.

We are not here to tell you off!

We are here to help you help yourself.

But you have to make a choice to make the best of the next ten weeks.

There are not many rules in this group, but there are some things we find very important:

1. Everything that is said in this room is private and confidential. We don't talk about them outside of the room.

2. We try to respect each other, to listen to each other and never to hurt each other.

3. If we have conflicts, if we feel uneasy with one another, we try to deal with them together, in this room. We don't leave the room.

We have a break halfway through the session, during which you can go to the toilet, one at a time.

The Name Game

Session advice: 1-2

Themes:
ICE-BREAKER
LISTENING

Aim **A playful way to get to know each other.**

Materials **A cuddly toy**

Description **Everybody sits down in a circle and a cuddly toy is thrown around to help rehearse people's names.**

Time **10 minutes**

Guidelines

Everybody sits down in a circle.

A cuddly toy is thrown across the circle while the person say their own name and the name of the person they are throwing to. The game stops when almost everybody is able to repeat all the names in the group.

Anecdotal evaluation

This is often one of the very first games in the group. It is a pleasant, playful way to start and helps the children to settle down, but also helps them to see the group as a playful event. One can see in the way that different children throw the toy about some basic group dynamics emerging even at this early stage. Some children will concentrate on the names while others engage more in the throwing. Some will throw gently, while others start to challenge the catcher or even try to hurt others. Some will take a lead, others will follow and others will avoid disruption.

The first coalitions between children, and between children and leaders, start to form. From this activity it is possible to draw up a first assessment of the group and its individuals.

Sometimes this game needs to be repeated in the second session.

Related activities

At the final session of the group we use the same activity, but instead of calling out other's names, the children have to say something nice about the person they throw to.

The web

A nice alternative to throwing a toy is to throw a ball of wool, while everybody holds on to the thread. The result is a web that shows the pattern of communication during the game.

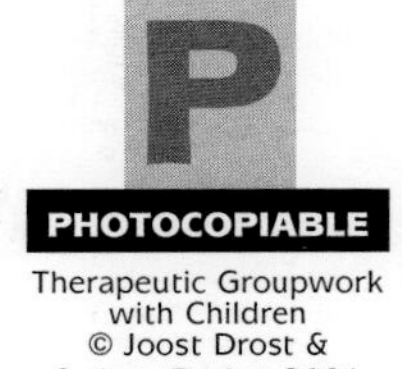

Climbing Up or Down the Tree

Ages 5 to 7

Session advice: every session

Themes:
- ICE-BREAKER
- IDENTITY & SELF-ESTEEM
- TRUST
- NON-VERBAL

Aim A tradition to mark the beginning and ending of every session and to link all the experiences in the group to a shared symbol.

Materials Worksheet

Description At the beginning of the session, everybody sits down in a circle on the floor or on their cushions. The first part of the poem is read out or recited together, while performing the described motions.

Being curled up – stretching and yawning – rubbing your face – climbing down – stretching and shaking the whole body – looking around and greeting each other.

At the end of every session the latter part of the poem is read while performing the motions.

Everybody finds their own place – waves goodbye – climbs up – curls up – looks around – dreams away.

Time 3 minutes each

Guidelines

Rehearse the poem together in the first few sessions to enable everybody to learn it and join in. The children might even be invited to take the lead. Invite everybody to join in, but respect their choice if they sometimes opt out.

Anecdotal evaluation

Young children really enjoy learning and mastering the words and movements. They often remind group leaders when it is time for the poem. Even those who do not appear to join in will protest if you miss it out.

Related activities

Most of the activities in the infant group will try to link in with this one, even

just as simple an activity as using leaf-shaped pieces of paper to draw and write on. More specific are the trust activities *Draw a Tree* and *Be a Tree*, the evaluation and group-ending activity *The Group Tree.*

The *Rap and Right* activity could also be used within this theme as a funny story to perform, but for younger children it might have to be livened up by strong visual cues.

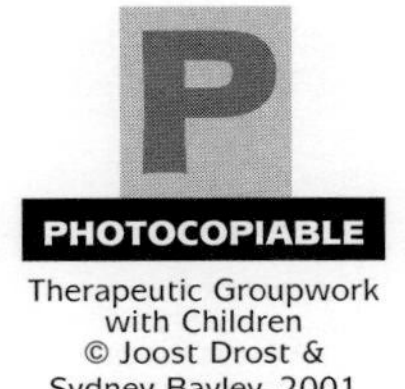

Climbing Up or Down the Tree Worksheet

START

Imagine a forest.
We all have a tree.
That's where we live.
The branches form a hollow,
that's where we sleep, all folded and curled.
Today we wake up, the sun on our face.
We stretch our arms and yawn.
We rub our faces.
We all climb down.
On the ground we shake our legs,
we stretch our bodies.
We look around us
and we notice we are not alone.
We are a group.

END

Well it is time to settle down and go our own ways.
Wave everybody goodbye.
Climb in your tree, higher and higher.
Settle yourself in the hollow of the branches.
Sit and watch, safe from your tree.
Sit and watch, calm and free.
Dream away, all by yourself.
It is good enough, just to be.

Draw a Tree

Themes:
TRUST
SELF-CONTROL
COOPERATION
NON-VERBAL

Aim — **A playful way to learn to work together.**

Materials — **Large sheets of paper, felt-pens or crayons.**

Description — **The children are invited to draw a tree on a large sheet of paper while they hold the felt-pen or crayon together. This can be done in pairs or in small groups of three or four children.**

Time — **10 minutes**

Guidelines

Get the children to work together in pairs or small groups. Place large sheets of paper on the floor that they can sit around. The children in each pair or group must hold the pen together. Invite them to work together, rather than with one person taking the lead. Challenge them to work together in larger numbers. Let them have a couple of turns at drawing the trees.

Anecdotal evaluation

We used this activity as one of the first trust activities for the infant groups. It is a new and quite personal experience for the children to work so closely together. Some children will want to dominate, others to follow. This exercise can be repeated in various ways throughout the group to see whether the patterns of working together will shift.

Related activities

The other trust exercises will build on the theme of working together. The *Labyrinth* exercise is a good step forward in paired working. In the sessions, this exercise can be followed by *Be a Tree*, in which the group sculpt a tree together.

Session advice: 1-5

Themes:
TRUST
SELF-CONTROL
COOPERATION
NON-VERBAL

Be a Tree

Aim — **A trust exercise that also helps the children to connect to the leading theme and introduces them to other, more physical, exercises.**

Materials — **None**

Description — **The children stand in a circle and together go through the motions of being a tree individually, being a tree together and encircling a tree together.**

Time — **5 minutes**

Guidelines

Instructions along the following lines can be given to the children:

Stand in a circle.

Let's all try to be a sculpture of a tree; wave your branches.

Now let's see how big a tree we can all be, if we join together, very, very close.

Now let's see how big a tree we can encircle if we all hold hands.

Anecdotal evaluation

This is a gentle way to work towards more physical trust exercises and encourages the whole group feeling. Young children enjoy the more physical exercises and circle activities, in which everyone goes through the same movements and takes turns.

Related activities

The *Circle* activity follows on quite well from this activity. Another activity is *Statues*, our group variant on a well known children's game.

The Group Tree

Aim

An activity that can be used to evaluate the group and to prepare the ending of the sessions.

Materials

A large paper tree on one wall and four paper leaves for each child. The tree needs to contain one piece of fruit for each child. If at all possible, make some fruit out of paper that the children can unwrap to find inside perhaps a small ceramic fruit or nut, which they can keep as a symbol.
Blu-tack® and pens.

Description

The children are asked to write the answers to evaluative questions about the group on paper leaves, which are then stuck on a larger paper tree on the wall. Afterwards they can pick a 'fruit' from the tree to take home.

Time

10 minutes

Guidelines

Give the children time to fill in each leaf. Invite them to read their answers out while they stick the leaves on the tree.

Introduce the activity as follows:

These are leaves for our group's tree, leaves about what you want to remember.

On the first leaf, write about what you have enjoyed.

On the second leaf, what you liked about each other.

On the third one, what you will miss.

On the last one, what friends are for.

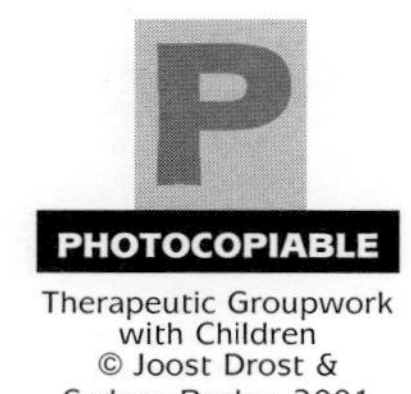

If you have finished, you can stick them on the group tree, while reading out your answers.

Once you've done that you can take a piece of fruit. This is the fruit that will fall upon the earth, that you will take away from here. You will carry it with you, remembering the good moments in this group and all that you have learned.

Anecdotal evaluation

This is a playful way to evaluate the group and work towards an ending. It helps the children to become aware of what the group has meant to them and what they will take away from it. If you run the group in a school, the tree might be displayed on a wall. The school could even end up with a forest if more than one group is run.

The children will probably need some help with writing down their answers. Children are always very keen to take something home from the group. Simple pebbles, nuts or ceramic fruit will have a very special meaning attached to them.

Related activities

The tree can in fact be used in earlier sessions to stick leaves on. Other activities which work towards the end of the group are the *Campfire*, *Losses* and *Feedback Certificates*. The younger groups also appreciate a party at the end of the sessions.

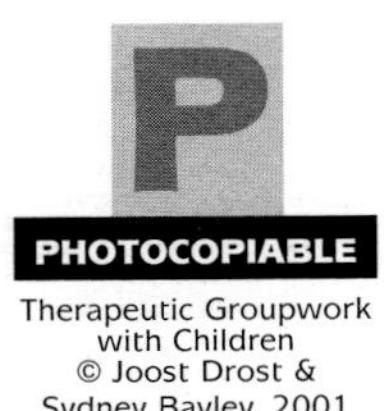

The Group Tree Worksheet

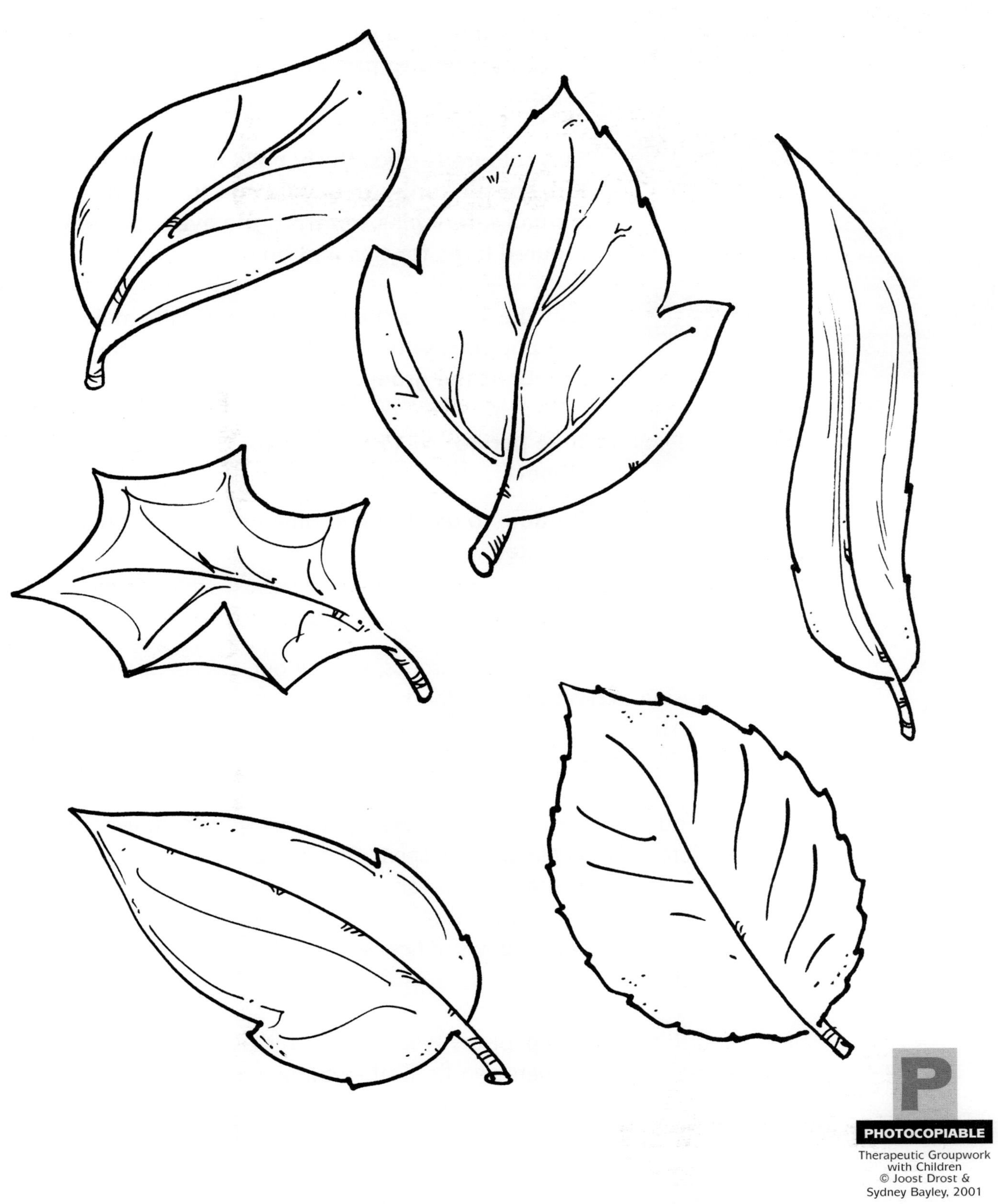

PHOTOCOPIABLE

Puppets

Ages 5 to 7

Session advice: all sessions

Themes:
IDENTITY & SELF-ESTEEM
EXPRESSION OF FEELINGS
EXPRESSION OF OPINION
COOPERATION

Aim

To help children to express themselves, to raise their self-esteem and to provide continuity over the sessions.

Materials

Plain coloured socks, fluffy balls for the eyes, red cloth for the tongues, needle and thread, proper glue or small safety pins to attach the eyes and tongue, coloured laces for ties and bows.

Description

Over the sessions the children gradually make their own puppets, which can be used to help them to talk about the group.

Time

Three periods of 15 minutes for the making of the puppets.

The time to use them in play and discussion is unlimited.

Guidelines

As group leaders in the younger groups, we use our own puppets at the end of each session to give some feedback about each child. When we do this for the first session we announce that the children will make their own puppets over the course of the sessions.

In the second session each child receives a plain sock. It has no eyes or mouth and therefore it is not able to see or speak. The group is invited to explore what the puppets can hear. The children can also take turns to make animal noises and the others must guess the animal. Afterwards, the puppets are individualised by putting on bows or ties, which makes them easier to recognise in later sessions.

In the fourth session the puppet's eyes are added. Make sure you have tried it out beforehand. Then there can be further games such as *Sad Tears, Happy Tears* and 'I Spy'.

In the sixth session we usually add the tongue and from that point on we can include the puppets in conversations, carry out the *Puppet Play* activity, etc.

As at the end of every session the group leader's puppets give feedback about the group, and their puppets can be invited to join in.

At the end of the group sessions the children will be able to take their puppets home.

Anecdotal evaluation

The children love to make these simple puppets and often cannot wait to continue with them. Making them requires patience, a lot of self-control and working together. It certainly helps the children's self-esteem to make their own puppets. What is more, the puppets help them to express themselves, both in non-verbal play and verbally. One eight-year-old child who continuously ran around and bounced on all the available furniture, transformed with his puppet on his hand and really started to speak a lot about himself and about the group through his puppet. Children who are shy and withdrawn start to explore assertiveness and aggression in their puppet play.

Related activities

We use several means of providing continuity throughout the sessions. In the younger groups we use the symbol of the tree and the puppets. In the older group we use various stories and also breathing exercises. It is also important to give all the sessions roughly the same structure and thus predictability.

Some other activities are related in that they produce something that the child can take home, eg, *Losses*, *Breathing*. Sometimes we also end up teaching the children to make paper aeroplanes and other paper figures, as some groups seem desperate just to have an adult to help them to learn new things.

Session advice: 5-9

Themes:
EXPRESSION OF FEELINGS
EXPRESSION OF OPINION
PROBLEM-SOLVING
COOPERATION

Puppet Play

Aim — **To free the children up in their verbal expression.**

Materials — **Puppets and worksheet**

Description — **In pairs, the children have to use their puppets to enact different situations.**

Time — **10 to 15 minutes**

Guidelines

If possible, organise a puppet stage, something for the children to hide behind while using their puppets. This will help them to really play without feeling that they are being watched themselves.

The children have to pair up and act out a scene. After every scene the pairs can change. Children can volunteer to take part or they can pass. Before they play their scene the children have to work out together what they will do, who will play who.

The situations on the worksheet can also be written on cue-cards and can then be drawn from a hat.

Anecdotal evaluation

Children really became engaged in this activity. Most of them like to perform, certainly when they themselves can hide behind a theatre or sofa. They allow their puppets to lose control where they themselves try to behave. In this way they start to explore what is safe and what is helpful.

By joining in as a leader, you can simply emphasise the important story lines that are brought up, by repeating the play. You can then sometimes introduce a more healthy ending to the same story. In this way you do not have to interpret the story or discuss it.

Related activities

What's my Line?, *Situations* and *What Happens Next?* are activities in which the children can perform and explore different situations.

Puppet Play Worksheet

Scene Cards

 make a friend	 have an argument	 sing a song	 say you are sorry
 make a telephone call	 silence the class	 be shy	 put on make up
 be very, very nervous	 tell a joke	 get home drunk	 ask somebody to come and play with you
 fall in love	 chase each other	 have a party	 improvise, make up your own play

Session advice: 3-10

Themes:
TRUST
IDENTITY & SELF-ESTEEM
CHOICES
NON-VERBAL

The Den

Aim — **To increase awareness of feeling safe and not feeling safe. To facilitate decision making.**

Materials — **Something to indicate where the den is, such as beanbags.**

Description — **A run-around game in which the children have to decide whether they feel safe and strong enough to leave their den, depending on what might be outside.**

Time — **5 to 10 minutes**

Guidelines

Make a den in one corner of the room, large enough to hold everyone. One leader can play the people or animals outside the den. The other asks the questions.

Play the game quickly.

You are all safe inside your den. Outside the den there is a tickling bear. Do you come out or not?

Outside the den there is a fierce bear
a dog
a ghost
a policeman
your uncle
your mum
your dad
your head teacher

Do you come out or not?

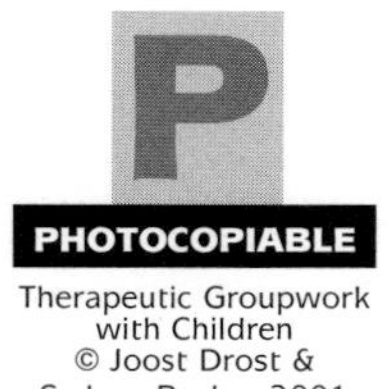

PHOTOCOPIABLE

Anecdotal evaluation

This activity came about as we noticed that the younger children were constantly creating their own safe dens around the room. As always, we felt it important to give them permission to do this and created this activity accordingly.

It is a very enjoyable game which combines making choices of safety with a rough and tumble game, which encourages group cohesion and trust. The children start to help each other to reach safety.

Often, the activity will end with everybody huddling together cosily in the den, talking about the things that have come up.

Related activities

Rescue Operation is similar in that children help each other to reach a place of safety but it does not combine this with choices about how they feel about different situations.

Situations and *What Happens Next?* explore how children feel about different situations through role-play.

Themes:
ICE-BREAKER
IDENTITY & SELF-ESTEEM
CHOICES
NON-VERBAL

Binary Choices

Aim **A playful way to encourage children to make choices and become aware of similarities and differences in the group.**

Materials **None**

Description **The room is divided in half. The children are asked a number of questions about themselves with only two possible answers and have to run to the side of the room that represents their answer.**

Time **5 to 15 minutes**

Guidelines

With every question the leader clearly indicates which group has to go to the left and which to the right. Half the fun is to play the game at speed.

Instructions

All those with brown eyes to this side and all those with blue eyes to the other side.
Dark haired and fair haired.
Those who have dogs.
Those who are good at numbers.
Those who like football.
Those who can touch their nose with their tongue.
Those whose parents are divorced.
Those who like pizza.
Those who see themselves as quiet.
Those who like dolls …
(and what about action men?)
Those who can stand on their head.
Those who like rain.
Those who sometimes lose their temper.
Those who have been to London.
Those who have a baby brother or sister.
Those who have nightmares.

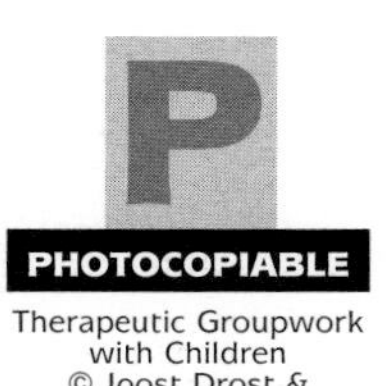

PHOTOCOPIABLE

Those who would rather be at school at this moment.
Those who bite their nails.
Those who are the youngest at home.
Those who like trees.

Anecdotal evaluation

Children like to have the chance to run around and take great pleasure in this game. They can also come up with suggestions to split the groups. Some of the questions are already more reflective and confronting. To actually physically move from one side of the room to the other helps children to open up and they are often encouraged by others who also own up to having tempers or other such difficulties.

The questions one asks are easy adaptable and this game can also be used successfully in more specialised groups, eg, around soiling.

Related activities

The activities *The Den*, *Opposite Sides of the Room* and *Four Corners of the Room* are similar in their physical use of the room and will give a certain familiarity after this activity. However, they focus more on expression, empathy and emotions.

The activity *How do you do?* is a more verbal and individual way to work on sameness and differences in the group.

Session advice: 2-5

Themes:
EMPATHY
TRUST
SELF-CONTROL
EXPRESSION OF FEELINGS
EXPRESSION OF OPINION
NON-VERBAL

Opposite Sides of the Room

Aim — **A playful way to encourage children to act, to express themselves and to empathise different situations.**

Materials — **None**

Description — **Children have to move from one side of the room to the other while they imagine and act out the different, opposing conditions on each side.**

Time — **10 minutes**

Guidelines

Walk slowly from the one side to the other, acting the conditions in that part.

On this side of the room it is summer, while on that side it is winter; just imagine how you feel, how you walk, whether it is nice and warm or freezing cold.

On this side it is ..., while on that side it is ...

stormy	calm
raining	dry
slippery	gripping
knee-deep mud	firm ground
snowing	sunny
winter	summer

Anecdotal evaluation

This is a good exercise to get the children into acting and you immediately get a feel as to which children like to express themselves in this way and which children definitely need some freeing up.

Children learn a lot from each other in these activities in which they all run around simultaneously so no-one feels as if they are in the spotlight.

Related activities

The activities *What's my Line?*, *Rap and Right*, *Favourite Animal* and *Rescue Operation* all invite the children to act.

Four Corners of the Room follows nicely on from this activity as it leads the children into expressing emotions.

Session advice: 7-9

Themes:
TRUST
EXPRESSION OF FEELINGS
IDENTITY & SELF-ESTEEM
NON-VERBAL

Ten Ways to Walk the Room

Aim A simple activity to anchor good feelings about the group in the way we walk.

Materials None

Description The children are asked to walk around the room in various happy ways.

Time 5 minutes

Guidelines

Ask the children to walk around the room at their own pace, in their own patterns.

Walk around the room:

hopping
on tiptoes
as if you have a string attached to your fingers
as if you have a string attached to your nose
as if you have had a really good time
as if you are walking on the clouds
as if you are really happy
as if you have made some friends
as if you carry a hundred balloons
as if the hundred balloons carry you
as if you are really proud of yourself

Anecdotal evaluation

We designed this exercise for a younger group that wanted to be on the move all the time and had really taken to the various exercises in which they had to walk around the room or go through a series of movements. By helping the children to recognise how different positive feelings translate in their own posture, they will become more conscious of those feelings.

This type of activity will be remembered as they use both the body and mind.

Related activities

Four Corners of the Room, *Binary Choices* and *Opposite Sides of the Room* all use the same principle of body and mind, ranging from easy physical conditions to elaborated emotional feelings.

This activity is best placed in one of the last sessions. Other ending activities are *Campfire*, *Losses*, *The Group Tree* and *Feedback Certificates*.

Session advice: 2-4

Themes:
LISTENING
EXPRESSION OF FEELINGS
IDENTITY & SELF-ESTEEM,
VERBAL & NON-VERBAL

Families

Aim — **To introduce the children to each others' families and put them into context.**

Materials — **Paper and felt-pens**

Description — **Each child is asked to draw a picture of their family and then, in turn, to tell the group who is who in their family.**

A variation on this is to ask the children to tell each other, in pairs, about their families and then report back to the group about each other.

Time — **10 to 15 minutes**

Guidelines

The children are invited to draw their families on a large sheet of paper. A pre-drawn house can motivate younger children. Afterwards, the children are asked to tell the group briefly who is who in their family. They are encouraged to mention all important people, even if they do not live with them. In the infant group, we will also ask them to draw smiley faces near the people they really like. The facilitators might comment on links.

Anecdotal evaluation

In practice, the children in clinic-based therapy groups often find this exercise difficult and may resist it or show their anxiety in other ways, by distraction or avoidance. Most of the children have significant experiences of loss that they have not come to terms with or relationship difficulties that are painful and can be defended against in maladaptive ways, eg, short attention span, attention-seeking behaviour, violence and aggression. It is therefore important to be sensitive to this and we often comment to the children on the fact that this exercise can be difficult for them.

It has also been important to bear in mind that we are bringing the outside world into the group, which is a boundary issue. This can have the effect of bringing in behaviour which we may not have seen up to this point. We tend to use this exercise in the third or fourth session. It is usually in this session or

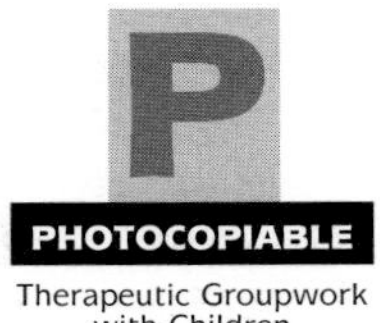

the following one that we see a lot of testing of boundaries and the most acting-out behaviour.

Related activities

The activity *What Happens Next?* explores how children expect their families to react in certain situations.

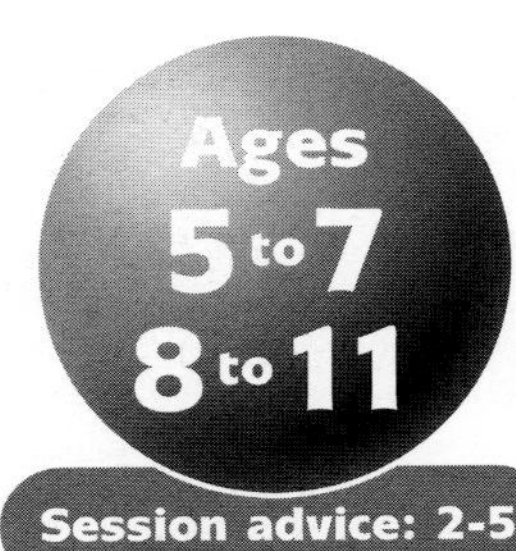

Session advice: 2-5

Themes:
TRUST
LISTENING
NON-VERBAL

Mirroring

Aim — **A non-verbal listening exercise, tuning in to each other and working in pairs.**

Materials — **None**

Description — **The children pair up and mirror each others' movements.**

Time — **5 to 10 minutes**

Guidelines

The children pair up and take turns in leading the game. Standing face-to-face one starts to gesture and the other acts as a mirror image, trying to copy every movement. Challenge them to try out exaggerated movements as well as very minute changes, eg, facial expressions or emotions. This can also be done in a circle.

Anecdotal evaluation

This exercise can be used both to increase trust and paired working as well as to make people aware of non-verbal behaviour and its importance. It is quite simple and relatively non-threatening.

Related activities

This activity could introduce other listening activities, expression activities and paired activities. *Funny Walks* is again a copying behaviour exercise, but involving the whole group.

Boxes and Bellies

Aim To build trust, cooperation and self-esteem.

Materials Cardboard boxes or beanbags

Description The children work in pairs and have to cross the room manipulating cardboard boxes or beanbags between their bellies and backs.

Time 10 to 15 minutes

Guidelines

The children have to pair up, although the pairs can be changed throughout. The children have to hold a cardboard box between their bellies, without using their hands, and make their way to the other side of the room. Next they must try to hold the boxes between their backs and return across the room. As a further option obstacles can be placed to manoeuvre around.

Anecdotal evaluation

This is a challenging game for the children and they often try out several partners to find the person with whom they can work best. Although this is clearly a physical game, it needs a lot of concentration and children are often surprised by own performance.

Related activities

There are several trust activities for both pairs and groups: *Labyrinth*, *Circle*, *Funny Walks* and *Be a Tree*.

Statues

Session advice: 3-9

Themes:
TRUST
SELF-CONTROL
PROBLEM-SOLVING
COOPERATION
NON-VERBAL

Aim — **A trust game in which the children alternate between controlling and being controlled. They learn to work together.**

Materials — **Cue-cards in a bag or envelope**

Description — **The children take it in turns to make the rest of the group into a statue. As inspiration for their statues they select a card from an envelope.**

Time — **15 minutes**

Guidelines

The children in turn select a cue-card from the envelope and sculpture the rest of the group into a statue, expressing the image on the card. Examples include a bridge, car, Easter egg, coffee, road, flower, pyramids, house, television, table, snowman, dog, washing machine, horse, whale and sailing boat.

With older children one could also use cards showing words such as friendship, love, fight, party, desperation or congestion.

Anecdotal evaluation

Children like the sculpturing game a lot and often position each other in funny, almost impossible, positions. The puppets can be used as part of the statues.

This activity, in which one is given a cue and has to make one statue out of a number of people is quite a challenge to groups. You could also invite the group to make moving statues.

Related activities

This trust activity emphasises group building. Children like selecting cards and riddles from envelopes and activities like *What's my Line?* and *Empathy Riddles* contain the same game aspect, which can bring life and motivation back into groups.

Statues Worksheet

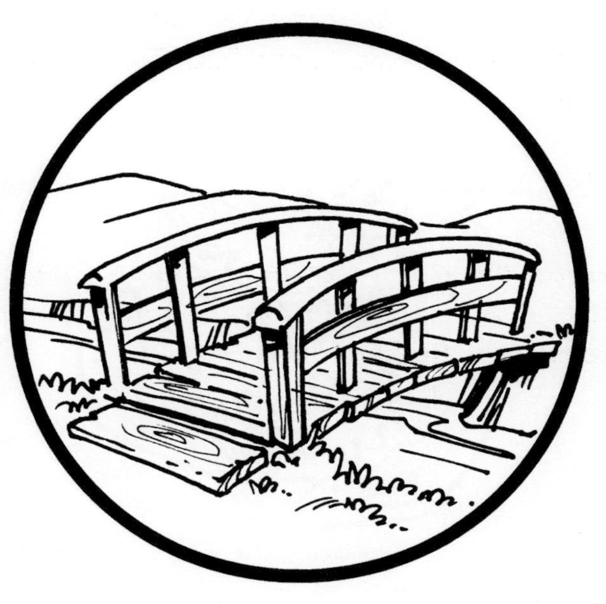

Statues Worksheet

Statues Worksheet

Statues Worksheet

Labyrinth

Aim — **This is an activity to build trust and respect and help the children learn to be perceptive about one another.**

Materials — **None**

Description — **The room is made into a 'labyrinth' by scattering the furniture around. The children pair up and lead each other through the maze in various ways.**

Time — **5 to 15 minutes**

Guidelines

Get the children to scatter the furniture around to transform the room into a sort of maze. The children pair up. One closes his eyes (self-control) while the other takes him through the maze, holding him by both hands and leading the way. Then they change roles. Next, one partner guides the other through the maze by standing behind him and gently pushing his shoulders. Next, one person leads the other by walking in front of him, facing him and humming, but not touching. Finally, the guide stays in the corner of the room and gives directions, eg, left, right, straight on, to his partner. It is good to do this activity with several pairs at the same time, which makes it more complicated.

Afterwards, the group can discuss the activity and explore how easy or difficult the various manners were.

Anecdotal evaluation

This exercise tells you a lot about the trust children have, their sensitivity and their ability to care. It can also create warm bonds between children.

We often pair up with one of the very insecure children, who gain a lot of self-esteem by being able to lead and control an adult. It is interesting to see how they use this. Some children need to be prompted or shaped to be more caring, which is best done through questions or role-modelling.

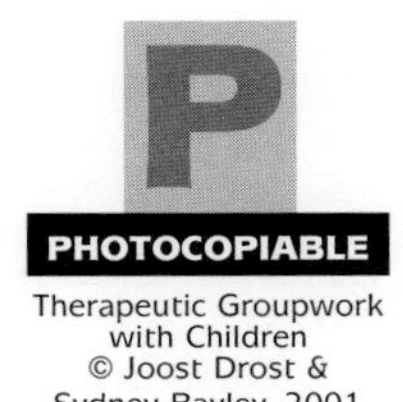

Related activities

The *Mirroring* exercise is a more simple exercise in which the children pair up and follow each others' leads, while the *Funny Walks* exercise is a whole group activity along the same lines. *Boxes and Bellies* challenges them to master a task in pairs.

Other trust activities, such as *Circle*, reinforce the caring aspects.

Funny Walks

Session advice: 4-9

Themes:
LISTENING
TRUST
IDENTITY & SELF-ESTEEM
SELF-CONTROL
NON-VERBAL

Aim A non-verbal listening activity, tuning in to each other in group format.

Materials None

Description The children stand in a circle and copy each other's movements.

Time 5 to 10 minutes

Guidelines

The children form a circle. One takes the lead and makes a gesture that everybody has to copy. After everyone has had a turn at taking the lead, the children start to walk in a circle. Then everybody takes a turn to invent a funny walk, which all the others have to copy.

Anecdotal evaluation

This exercise can be used both to increase trust and group cohesion as well as to make people aware of non-verbal behaviour and its importance. It is quite simple and relatively non-threatening.

One difficult variation is to ask everybody to adopt the normal walk of the target person and then slowly start to exaggerate this walk. This requires greater observational skills. Note that if the group has not bonded well, the children might feel ridiculed.

Related activities

This activity could introduce other listening activities, expression activities and paired activities.

Rescue Operation

Session advice: 3-6

Themes:
COOPERATION
TRUST
EXPRESSION OF FEELINGS
NON-VERBAL

Aim To encourage group cohesion and utilise the caring aspect.

Materials Cushions, preferably large ones

Description A dramatisation of being on a raft and rescuing those who are in the water.

Time 5 to 10 minutes

Guidelines

The children are asked to imagine themselves on a raft, with each of them taking it in turns to be the one in the water who needs rescuing. The others pull this person aboard.

Anecdotal evaluation

This activity arose out of *Operation Abandon Ship*, in which the children were to imagine themselves being shipwrecked. It is a fun activity in which the group can get in touch with their feelings of abandonment and experience being 'rescued' in a positive atmosphere. It encourages the group to work together in a cooperative way rather than the competitive way that many of them have learned and which can be unproductive. It is another activity which deals with loss and resolution.

Related activities

This activity relates to Chapter 3 of the *Bubble Gum Guy* book as well as to the activity *Operation Abandon Ship*. It also fits in with the theme in the activity *Losses*.

The Den is a similar activity where children have to decide whether to stay in a safe den or risk what is outside.

Circle

Ages 5 to 7, 8 to 11

Session advice: 4-9

Themes:
TRUST
COOPERATION
SELF-CONTROL
NON-VERBAL

Aim **A simple game about trust, caring, giving and taking.**

Materials **None**

Description **Everybody stands in a small circle and one person stands in the centre, holding himself relaxed but straight, with his eyes closed. He is gently rocked and moved around and across by the group, who make sure he doesn't fall.**

Time **10 minutes**

Guidelines

Everybody stands in a small circle. One person stands in the middle and holds himself stiff and closes his eyes. The group gently rocks and bounces the person around.

Depending on how much the person in the middle is able to trust and keeps a straight posture, the circle can be widened slightly. Every child can have a turn.

Anecdotal evaluation

For those who have never done this, it is a surprising experience. If the group holds together it feels like a gift, like being rocked or carried with great care.

For those in the outer circle it is a very caring experience, as what you are bouncing around is vulnerable and trusting in you. Groups often do not want to stop with this activity and keep on repeating it.

One variation on this would be to actually carry somebody around the room using the whole group. Some children find it difficult to contribute to the group and try to opt out. We never force anybody to join in. Instead, we would look for a more simple trust activity and work on trust in pairs first.

Related activities

The other trust activities, *Labyrinth* and *Volcano*.

Volcano

Session advice: 4-9

Themes:
TRUST
EXPRESSION OF FEELINGS
COOPERATION
NON-VERBAL

Aim — **This is an activity to build trust, self-esteem and to relieve anger in a playful way.**

Materials — **None**

Description — **The group stands around one person who squats and they press him down with open hands, without hanging on to him. The child in the middle has to explode his way out of the mountain. All children take a turn.**

Time — **5 to 15 minutes**

Guidelines

Just gently make sure that everybody gets a fair chance, best achieved by joining in yourself. This gives you a good opportunity to mediate the resistance of the group. The group often topples sideways, so make sure there is enough space. One can also use beanbags to create a mountain.

Anecdotal evaluation

The children like the challenge to their physical strength and also like to challenge each other. If a child is not strong enough to push upwards they will often find an alternative way out of the mountain, between people's legs and thus outsmart the group. In our experience this activity can often help to calm the group down. It is important that children learn to rough and tumble but even more so, to do it appropriately. We always comment positively on how the children are able carry out this activity and then settle down into a calmer one.

Related activities

There are other trust activities, eg, *Labyrinth* and *Boxes and Bellies*. It is good to be able to pick and choose whichever is most appropriate at a particular time. *Volcano*, however, is loved by the more boisterous children who love a challenge and from time to time need to release their energy.

Favourite Animal

Session advice: 3-8

Themes:
TRUST
IDENTITY & SELF-ESTEEM
EXPRESSION OF FEELINGS
EXPRESSION OF OPINION
NON-VERBAL

Aim **To encourage acting, empathising and identity.**

Materials **None**

Description **A guided fantasy exercise in which the children have to wake up as their favourite animal and explore how that animal moves, thinks and feels.**

Time **5 to 10 minutes**

Guidelines

Invite the children to each find their own space in the room and to lie down.

> It has been a long, long night and you have been fast asleep. Just think for a moment about your favourite animal. Picture it. Is it big, is it small? Is it furry, feathery, scaly? Is it strong, is it friendly?
>
> Now slowly wake up as your favourite animal. Think how that animal would yawn, how it would smile, how it would walk around, how it would eat and drink.
>
> Just move around the room, being that animal and ask yourself what it is that you like about the animal. Is it strong, is it fast, is it soft, is it nice, is it safe, is it exciting, what is the best thing it can do?
>
> How does your animal react to all the other animals in the room?

Finish the exercise by asking whether people recognised the different animals in the room, or whether they discovered something new about their own animal.

Anecdotal evaluation

This is quite an easy exercise for children. They really enjoy it and need some steering at first to explore their own animal, before they start to interact. It can tell you a lot about each child, what they value and how they feel about themselves. Sometimes you are able to use their favourite animal in later remarks.

Related activities

This is an easy exercise leading on to other guided fantasies such as *The Horse* and *2222!*

Other animal-related exercises are *Empathy Riddles* and *Rap and Right*.

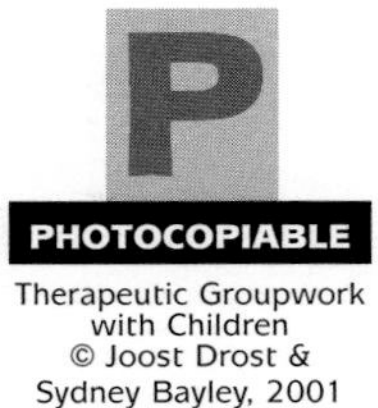

Chinese Whispers

Ages 5 to 7, 8 to 11

Session advice: 2-4

Themes:
- LISTENING
- SELF-CONTROL
- COOPERATION
- NON-VERBAL
- VERBAL

Aim — **A simple and well known game involving listening and paying attention to others in both non-verbal and verbal ways.**

Materials — **Leaf-shaped sheets of paper, felt-pens**

Description — **Drawings are memorised and then drawn by each member of the group and then passed around the group, to see whether the end result is different from the original. Then words are whispered from ear to ear, to see whether they have changed by the time they reach the final person.**

Time — **10 minutes**

Guidelines

The group sits in a circle. First one person draws a simple design on a leaf-shaped sheet of paper and the next person has to look at it and draw it from memory. In this way the design is passed around the group and finally the person who made the original design can compare the final result with their original. Several designs can be passed around simultaneously. Alternatively, words or phrases are passed, softly whispered into the next person's ear, to see whether they change in the process.

Anecdotal evaluation

This exercise requires quite a lot of patience but also leads to much laughter. The designs are easier, but they do help to convey that one can tune into others in a variety of ways.

A further alternative is to try to pass around combinations of gestures.

Related activities

Mirroring and *Circle* are other activities that focus on listening in non-verbal ways.

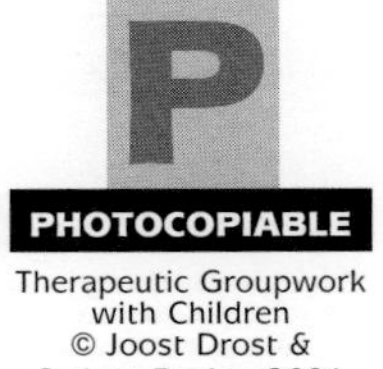

The leaves can be put on the group tree.

A good way to end this game and transform it into a trust game would be to pass the outside of a match box from nose to nose.

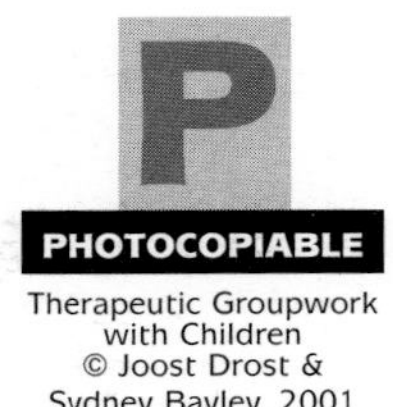

Magic Box

Ages
5 to 7
8 to 11

Session advice: 3-10

Themes:
EXPRESSION OF FEELINGS
EXPRESSION OF OPINION
IDENTITY & SELF-ESTEEM
VERBAL

Aim — **To encourage children to talk about some things, people and moments that have been very important to them.**

Materials — **A magic box. The simplest is a plain box that cannot be opened and has been decorated in an ornate way.**

One could also make a box wrapped in layers of different coloured papers, each layer carrying one of the questions. There could be a group reward inside the box.

Description — **A magic box is passed around the circle of children and with each round there is a different question for the children to respond to.**

Time — **5 to 15 minutes**

Guidelines

The group sits in a circle.

The box is passed around while the question is repeated.

If there are more wrappers around the box, one has to make sure that the box goes the full circle before the next wrapper is removed.

> This is a very special box. We will pretend that it is a magic box.
> In the box there are very special and personal things.
> Imagine that the box contains something you really want to have, what would it be?

Give everybody a chance to respond.

> Imagine the box could contain one person you would really like to meet, who would it be?
> Imagine that the box contains something that really goes wrong in your life, that makes you very sad, what would it be?

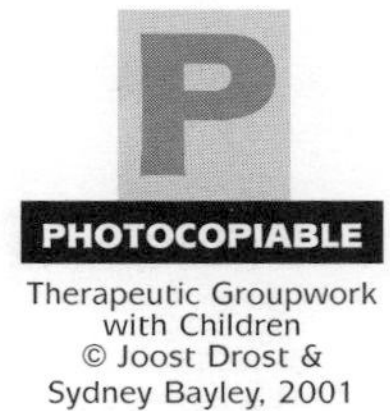

Imagine that the box contains something that you want to give to the person that you most love, what would it be and to whom would you give it?
Imagine that the box contains something that makes you happy, what would it be?

Anecdotal evaluation

This is a variation on a well known exercise. It is amazing how a simple prop can help children to express themselves. At the same time you should not expect great revelations. It is good enough just to ask the questions and get the children thinking in different ways. It is also good enough just to notice some of the more personal answers and not to over-react.

Related activities

Sentence Completion, *What Happens Next?* and *Situations* all help the children to express how they see the world around them and what is important to them.

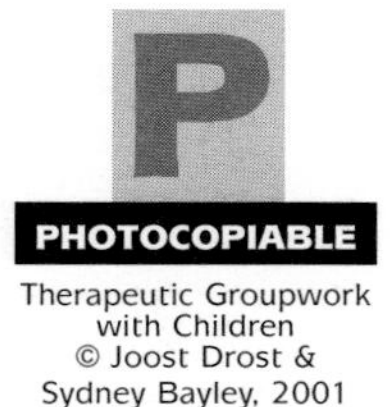

Sad Tears, Happy Tears

Ages 5 to 7, 8 to 11

Session advice: 4-8

Themes:
EXPRESSION OF FEELINGS
EMPATHY
VERBAL

Aim To learn about what eyes can express.

Materials A sad tear and a happy tear, either made from cardboard or two glass pebbles in different colours.

Description Two tears are passed around the group, symbolising sad and happy tears. The child holding the tear can name something that has made them cry with sadness or something that has made them cry with happiness.

Time 5 to 10 minutes

Guidelines

The children sit in a circle. The group leader explains about sad tears and happy tears. Then the sad tear is passed around once or even more often, while each child that holds it names something that has made him cry.

Next, the happy tear is passed around and the children name something that has made them very happy.

The children should be allowed to pass the tear on without naming anything if they wish.

Depending on the group, one can pace this slowly and more seriously or pace it quickly as a sort of brainstorm activity to loosen the group.

Anecdotal evaluation

Simple activities like this one help children to open up. It is not necessary to question the children in a serious way about their feelings. You run the risk of over-valuing feelings and in that way you might reinforce tearful or complaining behaviour. However, do not ignore the difficult things that the children might bring up, just note them.

Acceptance is more important than explanation.

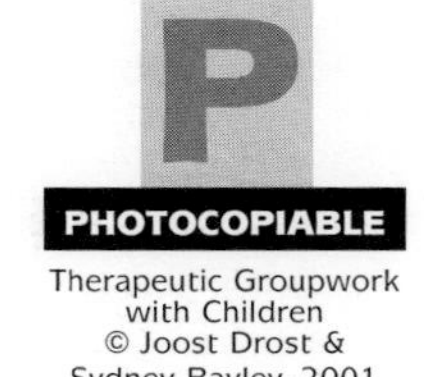

Related activities

This activity is played when the eyes of the puppets are put on, but can also be used on its own.

Losses, *Four Corners of the Room* and *Snuggles and Grizzles* are other activities that explore what makes the children sad and happy.

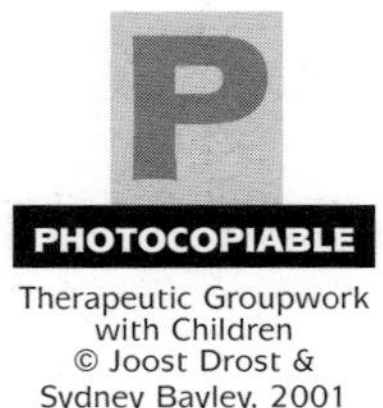

Snuggles and Grizzles

Ages
5 to 7
8 to 11

Session advice: 4-8

Aim To increase self identity, self-esteem and expression.

Materials Worksheet and pencils

Description A simple worksheet asking the children about things that are precious and things they cannot stand.

Time 5 to 15 minutes

Themes:
- CHOICES
- IDENTITY & SELF-ESTEEM
- TRUST
- EXPRESSION OF FEELINGS
- VERBAL

Guidelines
Read the worksheet together and ask the children to find their own examples.

Anecdotal evaluation
Emotional growth does not have to be complex and does not have to be therapy. Simple activities, such as this one about likes and dislikes, are as important.

Related activities
The activity *Bodies, Thoughts and Feelings* is a good follow up, with detailed questions.

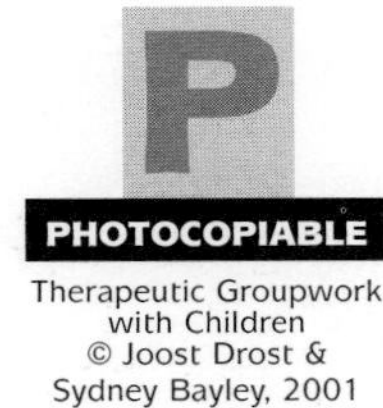

Snuggles and Grizzles Worksheet

Snuggles

Have you ever heard of a snuggle? Do you know what a snuggle is?

It is something very special and you, you probably have one!

A snuggle is something that is very special to you, something you never want to lose. A tiny thing that is precious to you and that makes you happy, gives you strength. It doesn't have to be special for anybody else, it doesn't have to cost a penny!

I have had all sorts of snuggles in my life. A shiny shell, which I found on the beach; it made my day. A pebble. My toy rabbit which has so many holes in it, but I like to carry it everywhere. An ordinary pen which belonged to my father. A tiny piece of pottery which belonged to the Romans, but I am the only one who thinks that.

I have drawn a few of mine.

Can you draw a few of yours underneath?

Snuggles and Grizzles Worksheet

Grizzles

Now you know what snuggles are. Can you guess what grizzles are?

They are things that you really hate, things that give you the creeps! But again they are special to you. Not everybody bothers about them. They are your personal grizzles.

Personally I can't bear chewing gum, I simply cannot stand the sight of it while others think that there is nothing better in the world. And I hate jelly. It gives me the shivers all over. And don't mention elastic bands to me, yuk!

Now can you draw some of your grizzles?

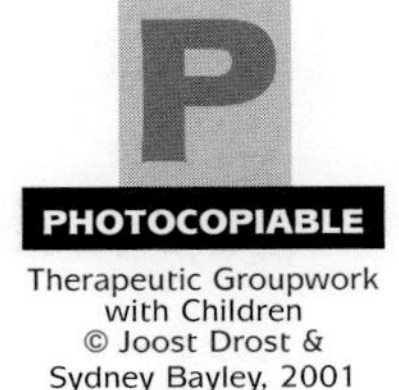

Snuggles and Grizzles Worksheet

A card game with snuggles and grizzles

If you draw your snuggles and grizzles on separate cards, you can play a guessing game.

Play the game with the whole group. Make one big pile of the snuggle and grizzle cards. Shuffle the deck of cards. Deal them out evenly. One player starts and asks another player to show their top card. The player has to guess whether it is a snuggle or a grizzle and to whom it belongs. Discourage the children from calling out if they see their card coming up. If the player guesses correctly, he wins the card and puts it aside, so that the cards can be counted afterwards, and he has another turn. If the player doesn't guess correctly the other player puts the card back to his hand and it will automatically come up again. It is then the others player's turn to ask another person to show their top card.

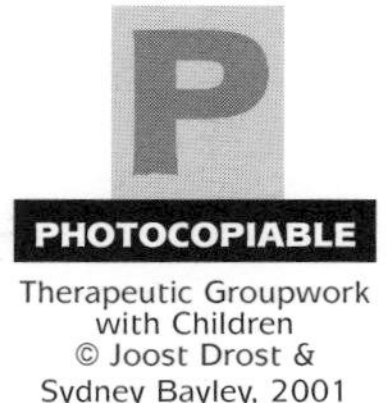

What's my Line?

Ages 5 to 7, 8 to 11

Session advice: 3-9

Themes:
LISTENING
PROBLEM-SOLVING
EXPRESSION OF FEELINGS
NON-VERBAL

Aim A game about empathising, thinking yourself in the position of somebody else, expressing and listening, observing.

Materials Cards produced from the worksheet

Description In turn the children draw a card from a bag and mime the profession on the card for others to guess.

Time 10 to 15 minutes

Guidelines

Get the group to sit down in one area of the room while the remainder becomes the stage. Invite the children one by one to take a card from the bag and to mime its content. The others have to guess what they are miming. The person who guesses correctly can have the next turn, but make sure that everybody gets a chance to play. If some cards are too difficult to mime, give the mimer the choice of either having a helper or choosing another card.

Anecdotal evaluation

It always amazes us how much children like to act and have great fun in this activity. Sometimes children are so detailed in their acting that one knows they have experienced similar situations; for example, one child acted being a nurse and was able to tell about his time in hospital.

One of the cards says 'teacher'. Quite often the child will stand up straight and pretend to shout. The group will almost always answer in chorus 'teacher'. Like myths, stereotypes have a very long life.

Related activities

One can also play this game with cards listing feelings. Furthermore it is a good introduction to the role-play in *Situations* and to the *Rap and Right* activity. *Statues* is another game where the children draw cue cards to direct the group in forming a sculpture.

What's my Line? Worksheet

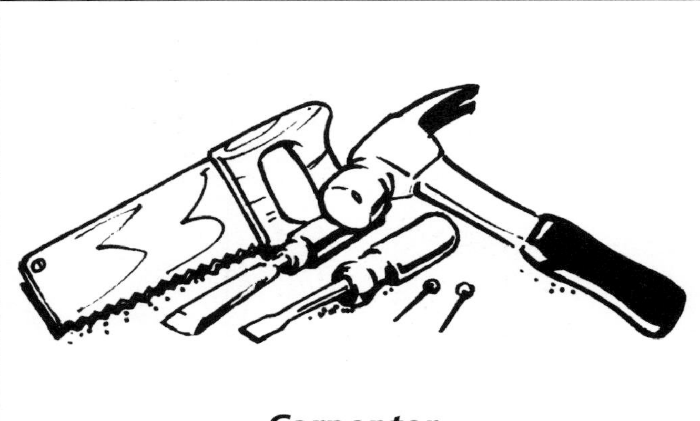 *Carpenter*	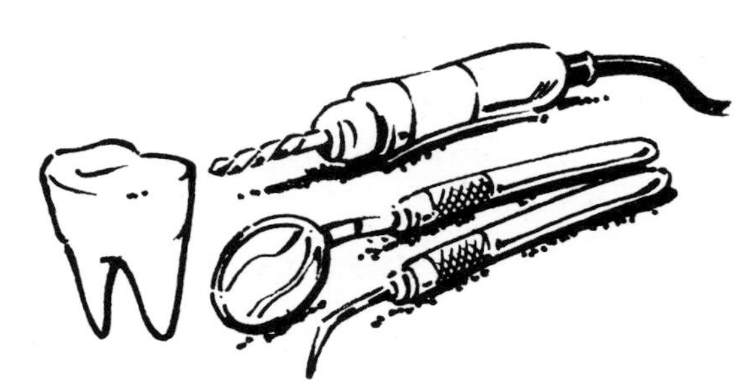 *Dentist*
 *Police officer*	 *Ballet dancer*
 *Painter*	 *Chef in a restaurant*

What's my Line? Worksheet

Clown	*Footballer*
Hairdresser	*Teacher*
Firefighter	*Shopkeeper*

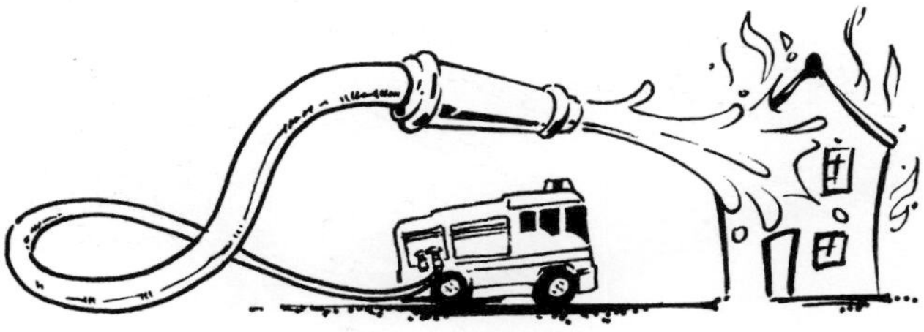

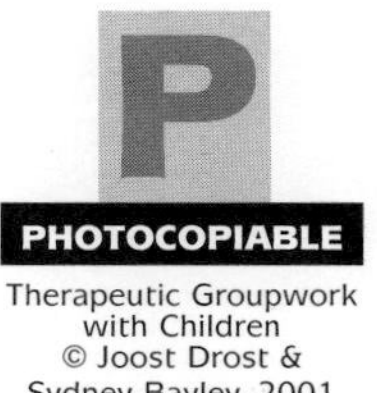

What's my Line? Worksheet

 *Truck driver*	 *Bricklayer*
 *Judge*	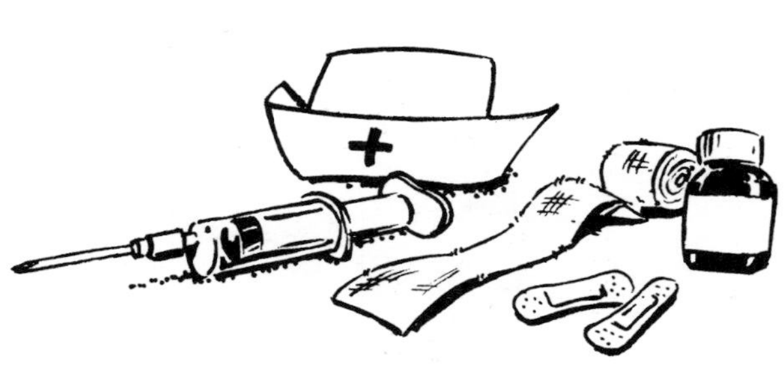 *Nurse*
 *Window cleaner*	 *Musician*

What's my Line? Worksheet

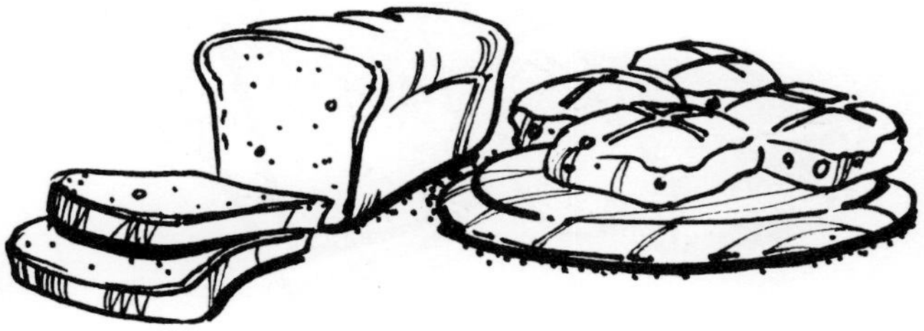

Baker

Animal keeper

Milk deliverer

Gardener

Ticket collector

Boxer

P

PHOTOCOPIABLE

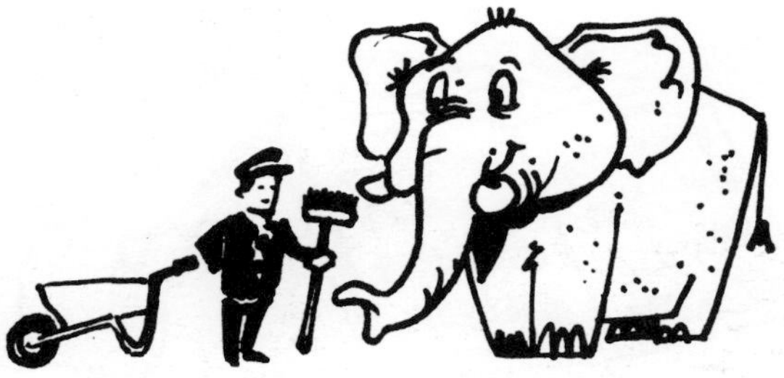

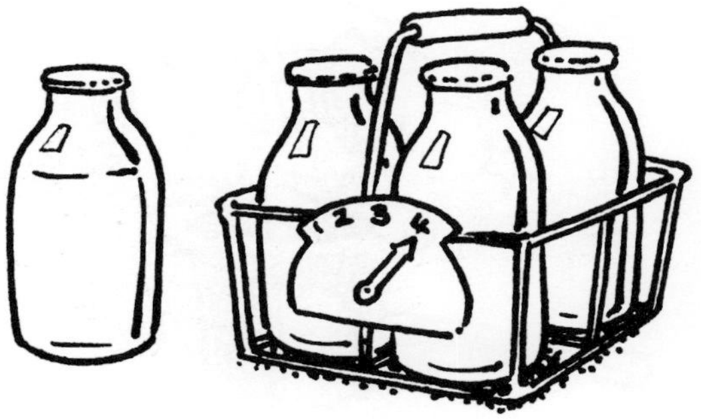

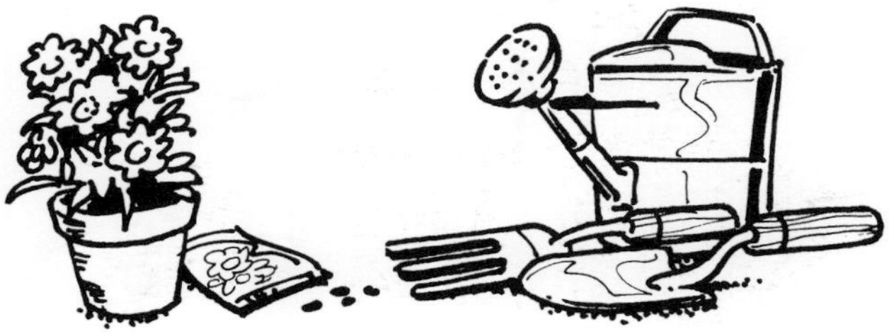

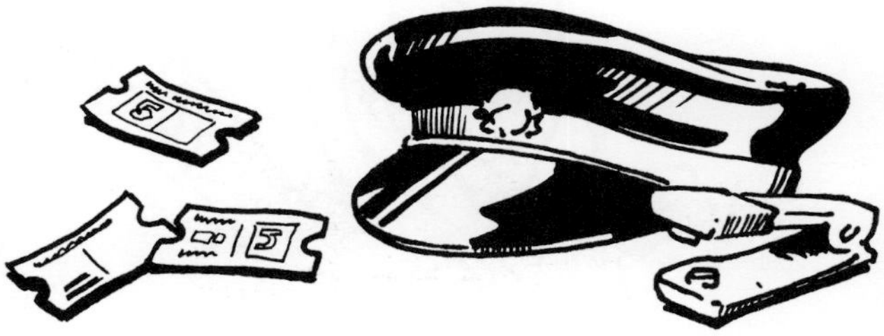

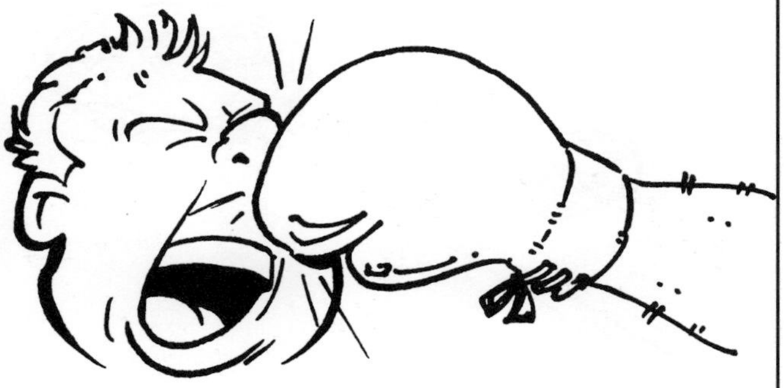

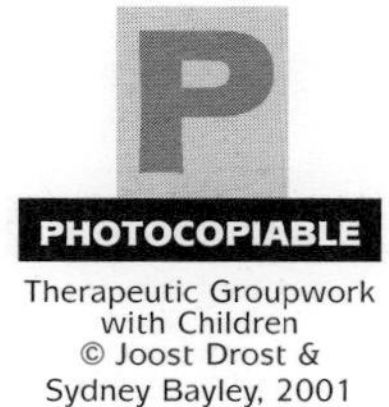

What's my Line? Worksheet

Choir conductor	*Referee*
Angler	*Magician*
 *Lollipop person*	 *Politician*

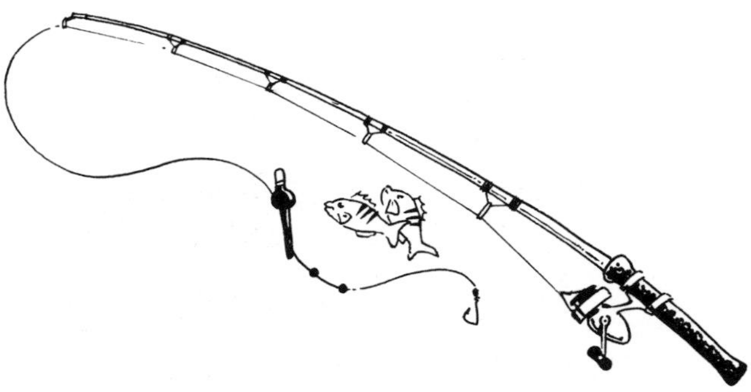

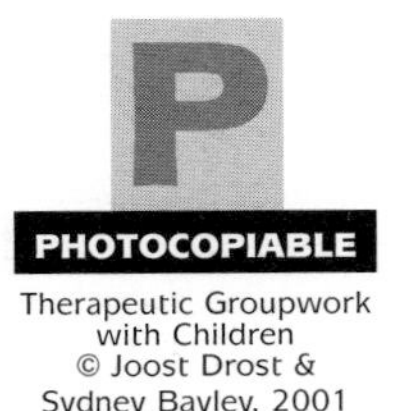

What's my Line? Worksheet

Writer	*Photographer*
Pilot	*Cyclist*
Swimmer	*Bird watcher*

Session advice: 3-9

Themes:
EMPATHY
LISTENING
COOPERATION
EXPRESSION OF FEELINGS
VERBAL

Empathy Riddles

Aim — **To invite the children to put themselves in another person's position.**

Materials — **The worksheet**

Description — **A collection of five line-riddles written from the perspective of various animals and professionals. The children work in pairs to guess which animal or professional is talking.**

Time — **10 to 15 minutes**

Guidelines

Pair up the children. Each pair takes a turn at having the first go at the riddle. They get 5 points if they guess it on the first line, 4 points on the second line and so on. If the pair cannot guess, the other pairs, in turn, try to guess and earn a point.

Keep to the original turn-taking for the start of each riddle, in order that every pair to has the chance to win 5 points.

Anecdotal evaluation

The children often like a general knowledge contest. However, here it is not so much general knowledge as empathy that is important. This means that it is not necessarily the brightest child who will be best at this game. This is good for self-esteem.

Children often ask to repeat this game. We have made up more and more riddles, but younger children also enjoy the repetition of the same riddles as they get a sense of mastering them. In some countries riddles are a traditional way of teaching.

Related activities

The activity *Sentence Completion* is about making your own empathy riddle about yourself. Children can also make up empathy riddles about other animals and people. The game *What's my Line?* is another guessing game, in which the children have to think for themselves how to build up a picture of a person.

Empathy Riddles Worksheet

Animals

1 I eat a lot and make a lot of noise about it.
I roll about in the mud and have fun.
I make snuffly noises with my nose.
I have nice big ears, which I can flap.
I have a little curly tail which I wiggle.

2 I sit upon my bottom and twitch my nose.
I use my front paws to eat my food.
I keep my food in a secret place.
I go to sleep for the winter.
I run up and down trees very fast.

3 My legs are long but I can't run very fast.
I'm as tall as a bus and make people feel very small.
I can eat leaves off very tall trees.
If I put my head down I have to do the splits.
I've got a very long tongue that I don't use for talking.

4 I am very nervous of people.
In some countries, I'm used for fighting.
I've got horns but I can't blow them.
I chew my food from side to side, not up and down.
I hate the colour red, it makes me mad.

5 People always give me a lot to carry.
They think I am stupid.
At parties you sometimes play with my tail.
I have been around a very long time, before there were trucks
I carried everything.
I can climb high mountains but at the seaside I only give
children rides.

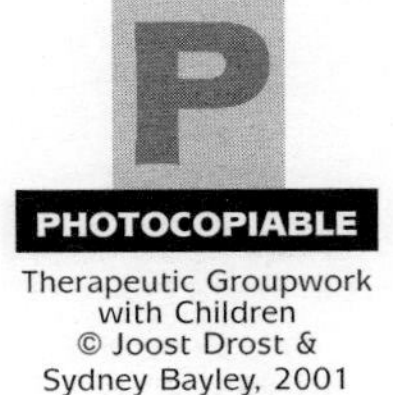

6 My skin might be thick and firm but I too can be sad or happy.
I do look strong, I can uproot a tree.
I always carry my own shower with me, be it with water or with sand.
If you tease me, I never forget.
When somebody offers me a treat, I pick it up with my long nose.

7 I am never lost.
I like salad, I prefer it to daisies.
But people put down poison, ashtrays or even beer to chase me away.
I hate birds and love cats.
They call me slow, but I challenge you to carry your own house.

8 I am very strong, but also a bit overweight.
If I scratch the end of my nose, I am always surprised how hard it is, hankies would definitely tear, if I blew my nose.
Everything on me is big, except for my eyes and ears.
I like running around, but I can't steer very well, nor do I manage the corners.
People hunt me for my tusk; I am almost extinct.

9 I don't need legs when I want to go very fast, I use my tummy.
I can be rather curly, but I am not very cuddly.
If I want something from you, I'll run rings around your neck.
I speak with a forked tongue.
I am not tall but am certainly very long.

10 I like a tarmac street, it makes such a nice noise when I walk.
Watch my ears and you'll know whether I like you.
Long, sandy beaches make me go wild, hold on tight.
I only have to dress up for a walk if you come along.
I am very fast in races, I like to win.

11 You can really get my hair up, and my back and my tail.
I am a very good at balancing, I can walk along a thin edge.
If I am happy and calm, I make a noise like a quiet engine.
If I am happy and wild, I am all over the place and up the curtains.
Even if I do fall, I usually end up all right. I've got a lot of lives.

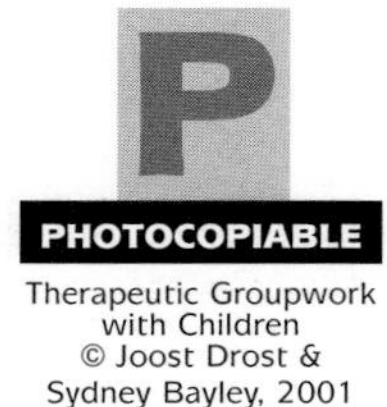

12 I can grab many things at once.
I am quite handy, if I may say so, or rather army.
I live in the sea but haven't got any fins.
If I could write, I could write eight lines at once.
I even make my own ink, but I don't use it for writing, just to scare you away.

13 Just because I look strange, it doesn't mean I am really scary.
I hunt by night and sleep by day.
I know that's the wrong way around and I even sleep upside down.
I am not a bird, nor an insect, but I bet you I can fly.
People think I live on their blood, but I really prefer fruit.

14 I know just one of your words and always say it twice, as it is my name.
When I call, you can hear it far and loud.
Children always copy my shout.
I even have a famous clock named after me.
I say I am clever, but people say I am mean, just because I lay my eggs in someone else's nest.

15 I am just very tiny, but quite strong and determined.
Don't make me angry, as I will turn rather acid.
We usually live and work in millions.
Together we can build mountains.
If you find it difficult to sit still, they say I might be in your pants.

16 Being big is not always easy, it makes it easier to be hunted.
As big as I am, I need you to save me.
Although I am big I am in fact very friendly. People like to swim with me as they say I have got healing powers.
You have guessed well; I live in the sea but I am not a real fish.
I have to surface frequently and blow air and water out of the top of my head, just like a fountain.

17 You had better not cross me, because I can be really dangerous.
That is quite funny because I am children's most favourite animal.
It must be because I look really soft and cuddly.
I am besotted with honey and don't mind the bees.
I often appear in children's books, I even have my own 'hundred acre wood'.

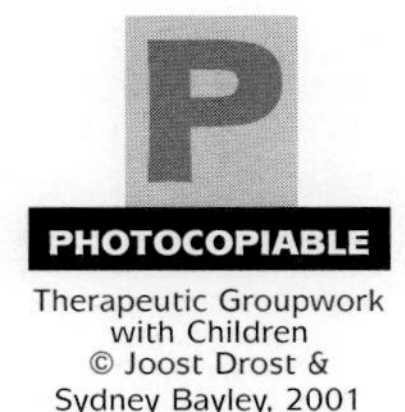

People

18 I have to keep children safe.
I want them to listen to me.
I don't like bright yellow, but it is a necessity.
I cross the street many times a day.
I can make all the cars stop.

19 I deal with a lot of money every day.
I have to take care that I have plenty in stock.
Most things I stack on the shelves, a few in the window.
Sometimes I have to watch people because they might want to steal something.
Before Christmas my job gets really busy.

20 I am on the road quite a lot.
People hate it when I am not on time.
I have to concentrate all the time, you shouldn't talk to me.
I have to be good at counting money, as I give change hundreds of times a day.
On warm and busy days my hands get sweaty and stick to the wheel.

21 I climb up and down ladders.
I ride on a vehicle that makes a lot of noise.
I am very brave and save people's lives.
Sometimes I cut holes in cars.
I have a big hose that squirts a lot of water.

22 I get up very early in the morning and start work in the dark.
I have to watch out for dogs.
I drive an electric van.
I have to try hard not to drop my bottles.
I deliver bottles to people's doorsteps.

23 I help children who are lost.
I try to stop fights.
I drive about in a car that makes a noise, with flashing lights.
I carry handcuffs and a stick.
I catch bad people and put them in jail.

24 I try to be nice but sometimes I have to get cross.
I write things on a board.
I work in a big room and have to keep lots of children quiet.
I mark books and hand out stars.
I listen to children read.

Answers

1 Pig **2** Squirrel **3** Giraffe **4** Bull **5** Donkey **6** Elephant **7** Snail
8 Rhinoceros **9** Snake **10** Horse **11** Cat **12** Octopus **13** Bat
14 Cuckoo **15** Ant **16** Whale **17** Bear **18** Lollipop person
19 Shopkeeper **20** Bus-driver **21** Firefighter **22** Milk deliverer
23 Police officer **24** Teacher

Four Corners of the Room

Session advice: 4-8

Themes:
EXPRESSION OF FEELINGS
IDENTITY & SELF-ESTEEM
SELF-CONTROL
NON-VERBAL

Aim To get in touch with and express feelings.

Materials Large pieces of paper, Blu-tack®, felt-tip pens

Description Acting out and drawing associations of the feelings anger, happiness, sadness and love.

Time 15 to 20 minutes

Guidelines

A large piece of paper is put up in each corner of the room labelled: ANGRY, HAPPY, SAD, LOVE. First, everyone walks from corner to corner, acting out each feeling as we come to it, perhaps doing this twice. Then each person, including the group leaders, takes a pen and draws on each sheet something they associate with that word. Afterwards, each sheet is looked at in turn and everybody says something about their drawings.

Anecdotal evaluation

This has been one of the most successful activities in terms of getting the children involved. It is good fun and we encourage them to be quite over the top in acting out their feelings. They usually have no trouble in thinking of something they want to draw.

The drawings can, of course, be quite revealing, and give direct representations of painful or good feelings. We deliberately chose the basic emotions, which everyone has and not the learned emotions such as guilt and jealousy.

The expression of these feelings leads quite directly on to the next session where we begin to look at the ending of the group by focusing on loss.

Related activities

Binary Choices, *Opposite Sides of the Room* and *The Den* are all activities which ask the children to imagine and act as if there was something in that part of the room, varying from physical conditions such as hot and cold, to emotions.

Losses is an activity that deals with more serious emotions.

Session advice: 7-10

Themes:
EXPRESSION OF FEELINGS
EXPRESSION OF OPINION
LISTENING
EMPATHY
IDENTITY & SELF-ESTEEM
TRUST
VERBAL

Campfire

Aim — **To encourage the children to reflect on what is going well for them.**

Materials — **Biscuits**

Description — **We use this activity at one of the breaks when biscuits are available. The children are given a biscuit for each good thing they can say about their lives, to a maximum of three biscuits.**

Time — **10 minutes**

Guidelines

The group sits in a circle with a plate of biscuits and the children are asked to think about what is going well in their lives and are told that they will be given a biscuit for each good point, up to three. They then take it in turns to tell the group.

Anecdotal evaluation

We introduced this, towards the end of the sessions, to see whether the positive feedback that we had been giving throughout the sessions was being internalised. The children sometimes find this difficult to do, and there are often aspects of their lives that are going very badly, but they are usually motivated by the biscuits and can find some things that are going well. These can be used as the springboard for moving forward.

We feel that it is important for developing self-esteem that the children are able to recognise good and positive things in their lives. Quite often, they are in a very negative cycle about themselves and what is happening at school and/or at home, and naming their beacons of hope can be helpful.

Related activities

An alternative, which we have often used, is to ask the children to say what they like about others in the group. Giving and receiving compliments is often a very difficult social skill.

The activity *End Game* is also useful for giving each other positive feedback.

Losses

Themes:
EXPRESSION OF FEELINGS
TRUST
LISTENING
IDENTITY & SELF-ESTEEM
VERBAL
NON-VERBAL

Aim To facilitate staying with and working through feelings of loss and making connections with the possibility of comfort and the working through of grief.

Materials The poem (worksheet). Plasticine

Description A short poem about loss and finding comfort in the face of loss, is read to the group. The children are then asked to make plasticine models to represent a significant loss and the comfort which was found.

Time 20 to 25 minutes

Guidelines

The poem is read to the group, it is important to have quiet.

Immediately after the reading of the poem, the children are asked to make a model of a significant loss which they have experienced in their lives. When they have finished, we ask them to make a model representing something or someone who was able to comfort them.

Anecdotal evaluation

The poem deliberately deals with the loss of a father as most of the children in our groups are not living with their father. It describes the feelings of sadness and of comfort that can be gained in a difficult situation. It is very evocative and usually has a tangible effect on the mood of the group.

This is a preparation for the activities which follow and we feel that it is best to read the poem straight through and leave it at that with no discussion. If a child does identify with it or express a feeling we acknowledge it but try not to dissipate the mood through talking.

This can be a very moving experience. Some children find this hard and stay with a quite superficial loss but, often, they will dig surprisingly deep and, in some cases, express something they never have before. Their models can be very detailed.

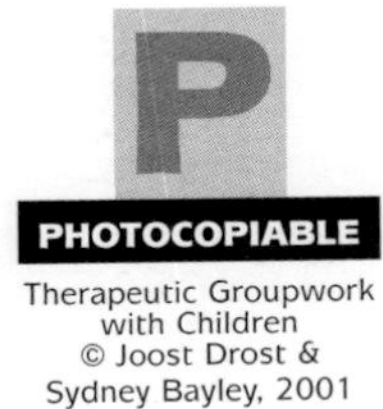

Our experience is that the children can get a lot out of this activity but it is important that the group leaders maintain a mood in which this can be done. It is easy for one child who is unable to contain his feelings to wreck it by attacking or making fun of someone else's model.

Usually, we use this activity in the penultimate session because we are close to losing the group.

Related activities

The Group Tree and *Feedback Certificates* both help to deal with the ending of the group, as does a good party, which we normally only hold for the 5 to 7 year olds.

Rescue Operation and *The Den* can both help to give a feeling of containment after this activity.

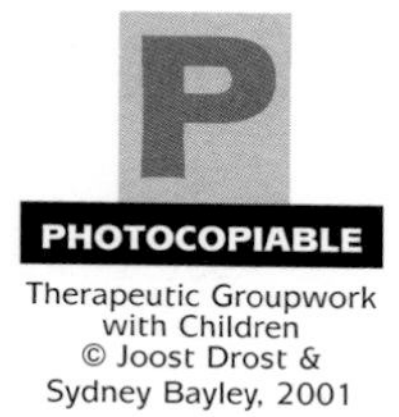

Losses Worksheet

My world feels empty
not the same
since my father isn't there anymore

There was so much I wanted to ask him
do with him, tell him
How could he, I was still so young

I pretended to be OK
to cheer my mum up

I now call it my elephant
People don't notice my sadness
my anger, my tears inside
They say I've got a tough skin

From time to time
I go to the tree at the back of our garden
It is my tree
I talk to it, it knows my pain
and when I put my face against its bark
it is rough like my father's chin

Session advice: 10

Themes:
EXPRESSION OF FEELINGS
EXPRESSION OF OPINION
EMPATHY
ENDINGS & LOSSES
IDENTITY & SELF-ESTEEM
COOPERATION
TRUST
VERBAL

End Game

Aim — **A playful way to say goodbye to each other.**

Materials — **A cuddly toy**

Description — **Everybody sits down in a circle and a cuddly toy is thrown around to help people give each other compliments.**

Time — **10 minutes**

Guidelines

Everybody sits down in a circle. Each person throws the cuddly toy while saying something he likes about the person he is throwing to. The game stops when everybody has said something about almost everybody.

Anecdotal evaluation

This is often one of the very last games in the group. It is a pleasant, playful way to end. It mimics the first group activity in order to give a feeling of coming full circle. However, the children now know each other and have more to say to each other.

There is usually quite a lot of variation: some children find it hard to think of anything to say, others say the same thing to everyone, while others find it easier. Saying positive things about each other (or about ourselves) is not generally encouraged in our culture so it is not surprising that children who have a negative view of themselves, and often take this out on other children, find this difficult. The group leaders take part and can therefore model appropriate things to say.

No matter how chaotic some of the groups have been and what kind of battles were fought between children during the sessions, this ending game is very important to the children and they are very willing to give each other compliments.

Related activities

We start every session with positive feedback about each child. In this way they focus on their positive behaviour and they also become used to compliments. Sometimes they will start to join in the process.

Around the seventh session we introduce a special break, *Campfire*. The children can have up to three biscuits but in return for each one they will have to say something positive about themselves or somebody else.

Feedback Certificates

Session advice: 10

Themes:
IDENTITY & SELF-ESTEEM
ENDINGS & LOSSES
VERBAL

Aim To give the children positive feedback about their contribution to the group.

Materials A certificate for each child, signed by the group leaders

Description A certificate is produced for each child, outlining four or five ways in which they have, in their own unique way, contributed to the group and/or developed during its course. This is presented at the last session. The certificate also acknowledges that the child has completed the 'course'.

Time 5 minutes

Guidelines
Each certificate is read out in turn and presented to the child.

Anecdotal evaluation
This is an important ritual, an acknowledgement of the children's difficulties and a recognition that the individual has taken part and has made a difference to the group. It is also an acknowledgement that their efforts to behave positively have been seen and heard. The certificate is taken away from the group, along with the complete story and the breathing graph sheet and other activity sheets, as a memento of the group.

The ending of the group can be a sad time and this should be recognised. Often the children want it to continue but it is important to hold the boundaries.

Related activities
Children like to take things away from the course. Apart from the certificate they will also take home their folder containing the stories, poems and worksheets that have been used. With the Bubble Gum Guy story they also receive a pebble and, if possible, the book.

The younger group will keep their puppets and a seed from the tree.

Breathing

Aim A playful way to increase self-control.

Materials The Breathing Worksheet copied for each child, felt-pens and a watch with a second-hand.

Description On a weekly basis the children have a timed attempt at holding their breath. They record their results on a personal graph as self-improvement is the most important factor of this activity.

Time 5 minutes, once it is a routine

Guidelines

The children divide into two or three small groups and sit down. The leader holds the watch, gives a clear countdown and encourages the children to stay calm and determined, but also not to overdo it and to know their own limits. Set a group limit of 200 seconds and explain that this is a safety precaution. In fact, the children that achieve more than 200 seconds are probably cheating, although we never point this out. Instead, we praise short but genuine attempts. However, you will be amazed at how long some children can hold their breath; some can genuinely exceed the 200 seconds. The results are recorded in the bubbles and graphs on the worksheets.

Anecdotal evaluation

This is an ongoing activity through the therapy group and is very much linked in with the leading story, which is about learning how to control oneself, through learning how to dive. The children like it very much and will often practise at home. This means that they will also think about the story and about the therapy group on an almost daily basis.

There is also the question of honesty, as it is easy to cheat. We always highly praise those children we notice making real effort and improving themselves in a serious way. It is good to talk about honesty and about the fact that the children must try to improve themselves and can be proud of this only if they know that they have made a genuine effort. This will emphasise the importance of the self, separate from any comparison with the group.

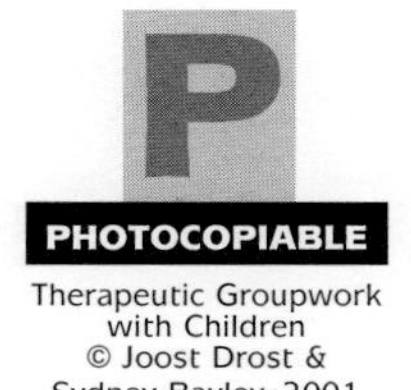

It might be that a more complicated way of analysing the results, as well as giving specific breathing instructions, could help to make this a more individual activity. For example, measure the lung-capacity of each person and relate this to the percentage of improvement. The magic of measurement and mathematics will make the task more serious. Children could be invited to invent their own lung-capacity measurer. You might even produce a small booklet containing breathing exercises (think too about hyperventilation and exercises to calm down), simple information about breathing, instructions to measure and results sheets.

Some people may be concerned about children with asthma and children who hyperventilate, but in all the groups that we have run, we have never experienced any problems. Children tend to know their own limits, and these may differ from week to week, if you are asthmatic. It is important not to build up group pressure to perform and compete, but to emphasise individual achievement. Knowing your limits and opting out of the activity are also skills and we usually give each child praise for their own achievement.

Some people worry that children use breath-holding as a means of gaining attention. We have not experienced this problem in our groups. We believe that this activity is unlikely to encourage breath holding as a means of attention seeking. On the one hand it has been turned into a game and presented as a positive achievement. As noted above, 'more of the same' is often a way into a child's uncontrollable behaviour. On the other hand, we make sure that each child gets unconditional attention throughout the group and therefore there is less need for this type of behaviour.

In any case the term 'attention-seeking behaviour' should be questioned; it may be that the child is seeking to participate, or to gain some control. Maybe the child is ambivalent which way to turn, like the cat that starts to wash itself when it doesn't know whether to fight or take flight.

Related activities

An alternative to this exercise is the next one, *Breathing for Diving*, described below. It is less easy to cheat and focuses more clearly on self-improvement. The *Breathing* activity can be complicated by creating 'difficult circumstances' like having to solve a puzzle, standing on one leg or answering questions. Mental activities actually increase children's ability to concentrate and hold their breath.

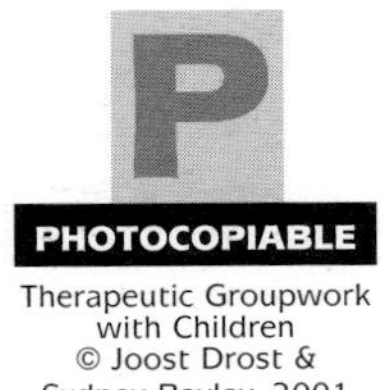

One might also introduce different types of self-control exercises, such as standing on one leg, taking only one nibble of a biscuit, musical statues, acting in slow motion, keep your body stiff, staring each other in the eye, tracing a line. Some of these might lead directly into concentration exercises. You can easily think of the benefits of using computers here.

PHOTOCOPIABLE

Breathing Worksheet

200
180
160
140
120
100
80
60
40
20
1 2 3 4 5 6 7 8 9 10

Breathing for Diving

Aim To gain self-control and learn how to relax.

Materials None

Description Instructions for a breathing exercise to extend the exhaled breath.

Time 5 minutes

Guidelines

Read out the introduction on the *Breathing for Diving* Worksheet or make up your own, then ask the children to sit or lie down and read out the breathing exercise to them. Try to ensure that not too much cheating is going on.

Anecdotal evaluation

Awareness of personal control is a very important life skill – activities in this area do not have to be complex, nor do they need to focus on just cognitive events.

Related activities

Any other exercise relating to control eg, holding breath, or counting to 10, getting angrier with every number and down again, from 10 to one, decreasing the anger.

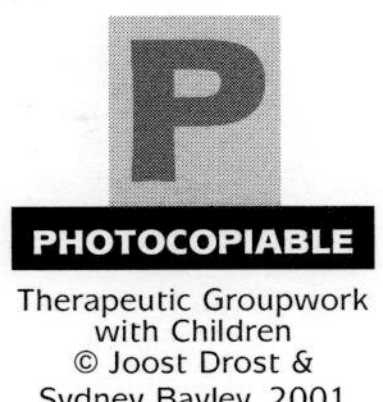

Breathing for Diving Worksheet

Introduction

Imagine you are on a boat out at sea. You are about to make a big dive to explore the seabed. You might be looking out for a shipwreck and pearls or maybe you will just be looking out for strange rocks and unusual fish. You are getting quite excited at the thought of what the dive might hold for you today. Just like a diver, before you begin your dive you will need to do some breathing practice to relax and control your mind and body – the sea can be a frightening place if you are out of control.

Instructions for breathing

Divers use special counting techniques to control their breathing as they go in and out of the water. They count 'one hundred, two hundred …' to keep time. This gives them control over their breathing so that they don't rush or go any faster than their bodies can cope with.

- Try to breathe in for 3 seconds. Count in your head by thinking, 'one hundred, two hundred, three hundred'.
- Next try and breathe out over a longer time than you breathed in for. Try it for 4 seconds, 'one hundred, two hundred, three hundred, four hundred'.
- When you find this easy try breathing in for 3 seconds and out for 5 seconds.
- When you get really good at this you might even be able to breathe out for 6 seconds!

How do you feel now that you have done this for a while? Of course, you can use this kind of breathing for more than risky dives – it can be useful on land too, when you feel cross, unhappy or out of control.

How do you do?

Aim — **A playful way to get to know each other in a variety of ways.**

Materials — **A question sheet for each person, pens. An overall question sheet for the leader to summarise at the end.**

Description — **Sheets with questions to ask each other in order to discover more about each other.**

Time — **25 minutes**

Guidelines

Everybody gets a question sheet, which can differ from person to person. The children walk around or sit in a circle to ask each other questions and they write the answers on their sheets. The questions are to be asked to all members of the group.

After 15 minutes of questioning time, everybody returns to the circle, with their forms. In turn, somebody sits in the middle or stands up and the others recount what they have found out about that person.

Anecdotal evaluation

This exercise is a good ice-breaker and stimulates the children to become inquisitive about each other. It asks them to use not only their verbal skills but also their observation skills. It is always interesting to see how the group organises itself. Some children will be very active and sometimes dominate with their questions, others can be more organising and will try to structure the exercise, directing the group in a calmer way. Others hold back, trying to find out as much as possible without actually questioning. They might be better at the observation questions. It might be useful to feed back on how the children behaved during this exercise. One could even make use of video for feedback.

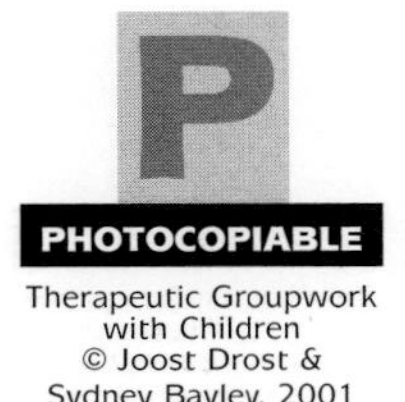

Related activities

You could also use the questions of this exercise to practice interviewing and listening in pairs. There are other ice-breakers, eg, *Name Game* and *What's my Line?* The activities *Operation Abandon Ship*, and *Operation Op!* are designed to get a discussion going in the group and to observe the group process and the roles people play within this.

How do you do? Questions Master Sheet

From this list several forms are built up with eight different questions each, two from each category.

A *Closed questions in which people just check facts and require yes/no. Find out from everybody in the group:*

1. Who has a dog.
2. Who loves sport.
3. Who hates swimming.
4. Who has ever been roller-skating.
5. Who has a girl- or boyfriend.
6. Who hates maths.
7. Who has been to France.
8. Who is afraid of doctors.
9. Who loves rain.
10. Who has nightmares.
11. Who plays a musical instrument.
12. Who is afraid of dogs.

B *Open questions in which people have to find out facts, preferences, opinions. Find out from everybody in the group:*

1. What their favourite food is.
2. What job they would like to have in later life.
3. What is their favourite book.
4. What is their favourite film.
5. What sport(s) they do.
6. When is their birthday.
7. One thing they are afraid of.
8. How many brothers and sisters they have.
9. What is their favourite topic at school.
10. What is their favourite pet.
11. What was their best holiday.
12. What they really hate.

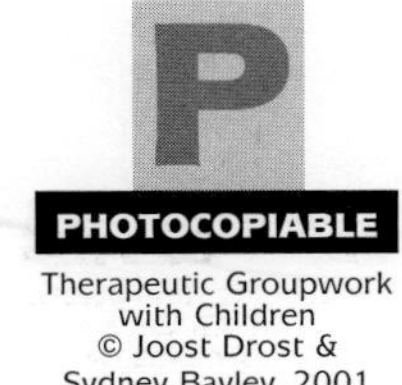

C *Closed observer's questions which just need careful watching of individuals, both about facts and behaviour.*
By just watching others, not by asking them questions, can you find out:

1. The colour of their eyes.
2. The colour of their hair.
3. Whether they wear trainers.
4. Which school they go to, without asking.
5. Whether they have any pen marks or paint on their hands.
6. Whether they have combed hair.
7. Whether they shout a lot during the exercise.
8. Whether they are good listeners.
9. Who sits calmly in their place during this exercise.
10. Who moves around a lot during this exercise.
11. Who seems to hate asking questions.
12. Who finds it easy to write.

D *Open observer's questions in which people have to invite the other to do an action and observe how they do it.*
Find out who in the group can do the following, by actually asking them to do it:

1. Roll their tongue.
2. Look cross-eyed.
3. Touch the tip of their nose with their tongue.
4. Touch the tip of their nose with their toe.
5. Split their fingers in two pairs.
6. Stand on their head.
7. Stand on their hands.
8. Whistle with their fingers.
9. Wiggle their ears.
10. Sit down with stretched legs and touch their toes with their hands.

How do you do?

Sample question form 1

1 Find out from everybody in the group, **Who has a dog.**

2 By just watching others, not by asking them questions, can you find out: **Whether they shout a lot during the exercise.**

3 Find out from everybody in the group, **What is their favourite food.**

4 Find out who in the group can **Roll their tongue**, by actually asking them to do it.

5 Find out from everybody in the group, **Who is afraid of doctors.**

6 By just watching others, not by asking them questions, can you find out **The colour of their eyes.**

7 Find out from everybody in the group, **When their birthday is.**

8 Find out who in the group can **Stand on their head**, by actually asking them to do it.

Names of group members

How do you do?

Sample question form 2

1 Find out from everybody in the group, **Who loves sport.**						
2 By just watching others, not by asking them questions, can you find out **Which school they go to.**						
3 Find out from everybody in the group, **What job they would like to have in later life.**						
4 Find out who in the group can **Touch the tip of their nose with their toe**, by actually asking them to do it.						
5 Find out from everybody in the group, **Who has nightmares.**						
6 By just watching others, not by asking them questions, can you find out **Who sits in their place during this exercise.**						
7 Find out from everybody in the group, **What they really hate.**						
8 Find out **Who in the group can look cross-eyed**, by actually asking them to do it.						
Names of group members						

How do you do?

PHOTOCOPIABLE

Sample question form 3

Question						
1 Find out from everybody in the group **Who has been to France.**						
2 By just watching others, not by asking them questions, can you find out **Whether they have any pen marks or paint on their hands.**						
3 Find out from everybody in the group, **One thing they are afraid of.**						
4 Find out who in the group can **Touch the tip of their nose with their tongue**, by actually asking them to do it.						
5 Find out from everybody in the group, **What is their favourite film.**						
6 By just watching others, not by asking them questions, can you find out **Who seems to hate asking questions.**						
7 Find out from everybody in the group, **Who has a girl- or boyfriend.**						
8 Find out who in the group can **Whistle on their fingers**, by actually asking them to do it.						
Names of group members						

How do you do?

Sample question form 4

1 Find out from everybody in the group **Who loves rain.**						
2 By just watching others, not by asking them questions, can you find out **Whether they wear trainers.**						
3 Find out from everybody in the group, **How many brothers and sisters they have.**						
4 Find out who in the group can **Split their fingers in two pairs**, by actually asking them to do it.						
5 Find out from everybody in the group, **What sport(s) they do.**						
6 By just watching others, not by asking them questions, can you find out **Whether they are good listeners.**						
7 Find out from everybody in the group, **Who plays a musical instrument.**						
8 Find out who in the group can **Stand on their hands**, by actually asking them to do it.						
Names of group members						

How do you do?

Sample question form 5

1 Find out from everybody in the group **Who hates maths.**

2 By just watching others, not by asking them questions, can you find out **The colour of their hair.**

3 Find out from everybody in the group, **What is their favourite book.**

4 Find out who in the group can **Stand on their head**, by actually asking them to do it.

5 Find out from everybody in the group, **What is their favourite topic at school.**

6 By just watching others, not by asking them questions, can you find out **Who is moving around a lot during this exercise.**

7 Find out from everybody in the group, **Who hates swimming.**

8 Find out who in the group can **Wiggle their ears**, by actually asking them to do it.

Names of group members

How do you do?

Sample question form 6

1 Find out from everybody in the group **Who has ever been roller-skating.**

2 By just watching others, not by asking them questions, can you find out **Whether they have combed hair.**

3 Find out from everybody in the group, **What is their favourite pet.**

4 Find out who in the group can **Touch the tip of their nose with their toe**, by actually asking them to do it.

5 Find out from everybody in the group, **What was their best holiday.**

6 By just watching others, not by asking them questions, can you find out **Who finds it easy to write.**

7 Find out from everybody in the group, **Who is afraid of dogs.**

8 Find out who in the group can **Sit down with stretched legs and touch their toes with their hands**, by actually asking them to do it.

Names of group members

Sentence Completion

Themes:
IDENTITY & SELF-ESTEEM
EXPRESSION OF FEELINGS
EXPRESSION OF OPINION
EMPATHY
VERBAL

Aim Self-exploration, self-esteem and self-identity.

Materials Worksheet

Description Six self-statements that have to be completed by the children.

Time 5 to 15 minutes

Guidelines

Hand out the worksheet and ask the children to fill it in for themselves, if necessary in silence. Some children might need help. Afterwards, you can either go through the answers with the whole group and compare, or either at this stage or later use the answers as empathy riddles and challenge the children to recognise each other in the answers.

Anecdotal evaluation

This can be used in an early stage to get to know each other but also as a follow up to the *Empathy Riddles*. Although it seems relatively simple, it is often difficult for young children. They might not be used to answering questions about themselves.

Related activities

This activity could be a follow up to *Empathy Riddles* and to *Families*.

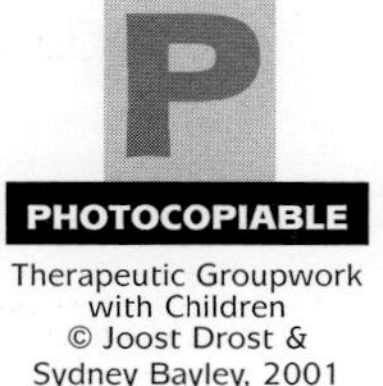

Sentence Completion Worksheet

When I get angry I ______________________________

____

____

What excites me is ______________________________

____

____

The best thing in the world is ______________________________

____

____

My favourite person is ______________________________

____

____

The thing that makes me most afraid is ______________________________

____

____

P

PHOTOCOPIABLE

What Happens Next?

Ages 8 to 11

Session advice: 4-8

Themes:
- EXPRESSION OF FEELINGS
- EXPRESSION OF OPINION
- IDENTITY & SELF-ESTEEM
- PROBLEM-SOLVING
- SELF-CONTROL
- VERBAL

Aim **To explore the perceptions children have about themselves, their parents or carers and others.**

Materials **Worksheets with written story stems and questions to be filled in by the children.**

Description **The children are given a number of story stems about everyday potentially confrontational situations and have to complete questions about what they think might happen next.**

Time **15 to 20 minutes**

Guidelines

With older children, the worksheets can be handed out and they can fill in the answers for themselves. If the group has difficulties in reading and writing, it is easier to go through them together and compare the answers. It might also be helpful to act the situations out.

There are a number of scenarios in this exercise, which permits you to divide it and spread it over more sessions.

Anecdotal evaluation

This is a helpful means of encouraging self-reflection in written form. With 8 to 11 years olds, you cannot expect long answers. However, the answers tell you a lot about their important relationships in life, and how they expect to be approached by their parents, peers and teachers. People's lives tend to run along dominant storylines, eg, a child always feeling blamed for everything by his parents. This will, of course, influence their behaviour towards their parents.

Going through the stories as a group will bring up different storylines and might help the children to discover how they can deal with confrontational situations differently.

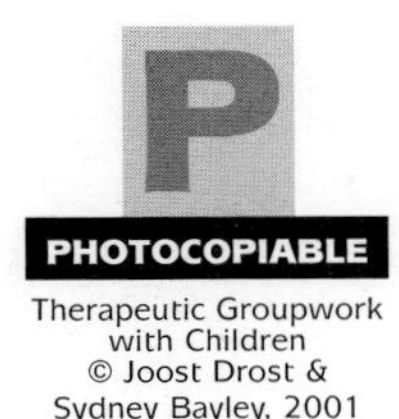

Related activities

This activity is very similar to *Situations* and can be used almost in the same way. The written form might be more helpful for some and easier to apply in whole class situations. You could even combine this with a maths exercise involving making graphs or bar charts. Plot how many children give a similar type of answer to a situation. This is an example of how positive mental health activities can be combined with National Curriculum requirements.

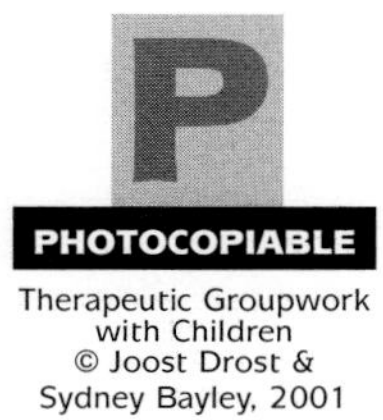

What Happens Next? Worksheet

How well do we know others and ourselves?

Imagine yourself in the following situations and think about how you and the other might react.

You are standing in the playground and a classmate keeps staring at you, with a rather empty expression, not angry but not smiling either.
What will you think, feel, say and do?

____

____

____

You have just got a new bike and you want to give it a try. Your parents warn you to be careful on the road. Then a big truck speeds up the road behind you and you panic and crash into a hedge. You only hurt your knee and cut your hand.
What will your parents say and do?

____

____

____

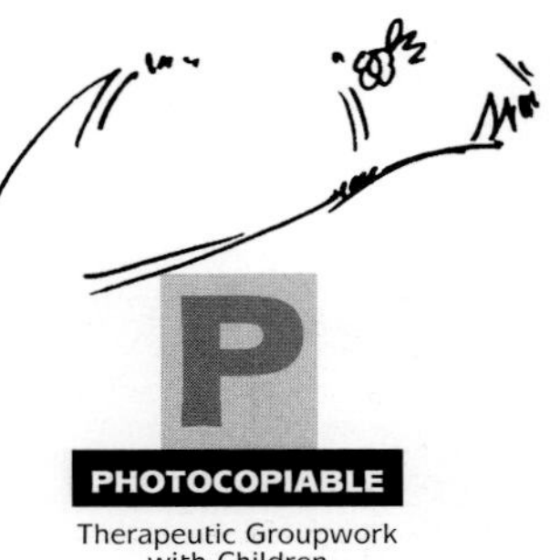

You are walking home from school with a classmate. You are thinking about an argument you had with your mum that morning, when your classmate asks you whether you have any stickers to swap. You don't answer, in fact, you probably don't even hear the question. But your classmate reacts angrily: 'Well, you're thick. If you can't be bothered to tell me, you'll never get anything from me again!'

What will you think, feel, say and do?

Your whole family has overslept and you had to rush to school. You made it just in time, but forgot to bring your reading-book and you know that your teacher wants to read with you today.

What will your teacher say and do?

Your parents are clearly annoyed. They slam doors, shout and can't be bothered to listen to you.

What will you think, feel, say and do?

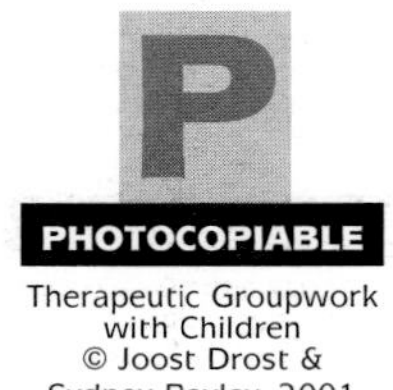

PHOTOCOPIABLE

Your teacher has given you a major detention. According to her you were rude to her.

What will your parents say and do?

You have made something special at school for your mum. After all it is mother's day. But when you give it to her, she is not paying any attention and says 'Can't you see that I am busy working?'

What will you think, feel, say and do?

You took your sticker-book to school. While in class, one of the other children grabs one of the stickers, so you try to pull it out of his hands.

What will the teacher say?

Your classmates have been making fun of you after school. When you ran after them, you fell and ripped your school trousers. They laughed even more and ran off.

What will your parents say and do?

Your dad is cooking and you want to know what's in the pots. He warns you not to touch them. When you lift one of the lids, you knock the hot gravy over and some of it spills over your hands.

How will your dad react? If it had been your mum, would she have reacted any differently?

On a rainy afternoon you have had fun making a little truck out of paper, card and glue. You leave it in on the sofa. Your dad arrives home from work, tired as he always is, and drops himself on the sofa and squashes your truck, still wet from the glue.

What will happen next?

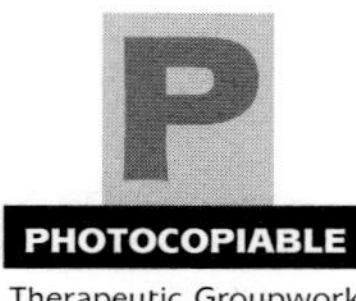

Your mum is furious because you have accidentally broken her favourite vase, flowers and all!

What will you do, say and feel?

____

____

____

You come home from school, throw your bag in the corner and rush out to play. Your mum stops you and asks 'What about your homework?' As you are almost out of the door you answer 'Oh, we haven't got any'.

What will your mum say and what will she do?

____

____

____

Yesterday you had a big row with your parents as you didn't want to go to bed and it took you hours to get your pyjamas on … your parents were furious. It's nearly bedtime now but you really want to watch the end of the movie. After all, it will only be half an hour later than your normal bedtime.

What will you do?

____

____

____

You are watching your favourite cartoon on the only working television in the house. Your dad comes in and wants to watch a football match on the other channel. You get angry and yell at him 'You always have things your way!'

What will your dad do?

You get into a fight at school and get suspended.

How will your parents react?

You've been lucky, you and your dad won £10 in the Lottery on Saturday and you were allowed to spend it all. When you tell your classmates about it in the playground, one calls you a 'stupid liar'.

What will you say? What will you do?

Two classmates are standing in the playground. Just as you pass them they burst out laughing.

What will you think, what will you do?

Situations

Ages 8 to 11

Session advice: 4-8

Themes:
- CHOICES
- IDENTITY & SELF-ESTEEM
- PROBLEM-SOLVING
- EXPRESSION OF OPINION
- VERBAL

Aim To explore different solutions to everyday situations where faulty perceptions may have led to misunderstanding and over-reaction.

Materials Worksheet

Description We have written a number of scripts for everyday situations which can be role-played with alternative endings. These can be played by the children or the group leaders, but the children are encouraged to look for different solutions to the dilemmas that are contained within the stories.

Time 15 to 20 minutes

Guidelines

The worksheet gives four different situations to be played by two or three children. The children are each given a piece of paper from the worksheet that explains their role. They have to keep it secret as the other players have their own instructions. They are asked to act out their different roles, to see how the situation is resolved. Alternatively, the facilitators can act out the situation. The whole group is then asked what has happened and how it seemed that the characters were feeling and also to suggest different and better solutions that leave both parties feeling OK.

Anecdotal evaluation

We have found this to be an effective way of challenging common misperceptions about everyday situations that can lead to unacceptable behaviour, eg, believing that someone who is upset is upset with you, rather than considering that it might be about something else that has happened earlier. One of our most important general aims is to encourage the children to think about their behaviour rather than to react on impulse and this is one of the activities that is useful in achieving that aim.

We have found that groups vary greatly as to whether they can use role-play effectively. Our original intention was to ask the children to carry out the role-play about themselves but in some groups we have found it more effective to

do it ourselves. The task does depend on the children being able to stay in role without it becoming so real that they cannot differentiate and begin to act out their own conflicts, in reality, within the group.

Related activities

The activities *Operation Abandon Ship* and *Operation Op!* invite children to take on roles and explore a new problem. The activity *What Happens Next?* explores situations in a written question format and can also be used for role-play.

Situations Worksheet

1 A *You play yourself.*
You have just been out playing in the fields, a couple of streets away. A hot air balloon landed and you were asked to help to pack it away. You even earned some money. When you come home you find your dad in the kitchen, preparing the tea and you can't wait to tell him the whole story.

Start by opening the kitchen door and entering the kitchen.

1 B *You play a dad.*
You had an awful day. To begin with you woke up with a headache. Then everything went wrong. Your son's dog messed in the living room; there were bills in the post that you don't know how you are going to pay, and the washing machine broke down. On top of everything it is getting dark and your son is over an hour late. You are very worried, angry, dead tired and fed up.

You are in the kitchen, peeling potatoes, when your son comes in.

2 A *You play yourself.*
Before school you meet a friend in the playground. Yesterday you had a race with him and he lost. You greet him like you do every morning.

2 B *You play yourself.*
Your mum has suddenly become quite ill and had to be rushed to hospital in the middle of the night. You had to go to school anyway as your dad couldn't have you at home. You are worried about your mum and can't think about anything else.

In the playground you don't feel like talking to anybody, even your best friend. It seems easier to walk away from people than to talk to them.

3 A *You play yourself.*
Because you watched a late-night movie last night, you overslept this morning. You had to hurry but you did make it in time to school. Only you have forgotten your PE bag, which you need for the very first lesson.

3 B *You play a PE teacher.*
It is the beginning of a school day; first lesson. One of your pupils has forgotten his PE bag. You ask him in a neutral, neither angry nor friendly, way: 'Can you explain to me why you didn't remember to bring your PE bag today?'.

4 A *2 players. You play yourselves.*
The two of you are standing in the playground and you are playing a game where you are holding hands and pull each other backwards and forwards. When a classmate approaches, one of you accidentally stumbles into him. Don't hurt anybody.

4 B *You play yourself.*
In the playground you go up to two classmates who are playing some kind of game. You intend to ask them whether they have found your pack of football stickers.

Operation Abandon Ship

Ages 8 to 11

Session advice: 3-7

Themes:
- LISTENING
- CHOICES
- PROBLEM-SOLVING
- EXPRESSION OF OPINION
- COOPERATION
- VERBAL

Aim **A team-building activity in which the children first have to make their own choices and then have to organise themselves to reach a group decision. Very suitable for (video) feedback on people's roles in groups.**

Materials **The worksheet. With younger children the pictures of the items could be cut out.**

Description **The group is presented with the worksheet which places them in a fantasy situation on a sinking ship. From a list of 20 items they first have to pick their own top five items needed for survival on a desert island. They then have to negotiate a group decision about which five items to save.**

Time **15 to 20 minutes**

Guidelines

Hand out the worksheet and read it aloud together. It might be helpful to actually draw the location of the ship and the island in the room. Read the list of items together, and then give the children five minutes to make their own choices, in silence. They have to prioritise their five items, giving five points to the item they value most, four points for the second best, etc. Then give them ten minutes to come to a group decision. Don't intervene, just remind them that the boat is slowly sinking.

By multiplying each person's priority score for each item with the group score for that item and totalling those figures, one can discover who had the largest input into the final group score.

Option: 'The Test', a number of questions for the children to evaluate whether their items were any use at all.

One should not underestimate the skills required for this task. For younger

groups we advise not using the points system and instead making illustrated cards showing the objects, to allow the children to select their five items manually.

Anecdotal evaluation

This activity is very interesting to observe, as people quickly take different roles in the process. It allows you to give detailed feedback on how the children contribute. Often one child shouts the loudest but the others will take the process forward through constructive ideas and by questioning each other and listening to their answers. If you have the opportunity, video-tape this activity and watch it together.

Related activities

Activity *Operation Op!* is about making choices, but this time about prioritising people for treatment; it is more suitable for older children.

A simple, introductory activity on making choices is *Binary Choices*.

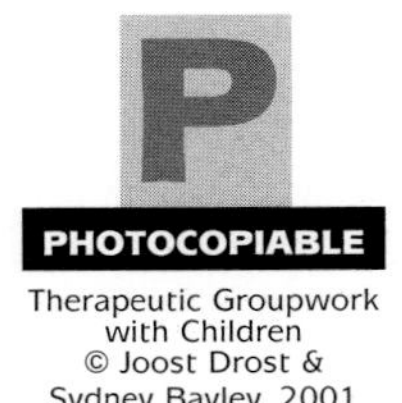

Operation Abandon Ship Worksheet

Imagine:

As a group you are sailing around the world. Your ship is packed with tinned food and a super built-in kitchen ...

But, a storm throws you onto a rock and you have about 15 minutes before the ship is torn to pieces.

Nearby is a small deserted island, within swimming distance. Each of you can take along one bag of tinned food and one of the other items listed. Only one, no matter what its size!

First, prioritise the five items on the list that you would choose for the whole group to take to the island and think about the reasons why you would need them. Give 5 points to the item you value most, 4 points to the next one and so on.

After everybody has made up their own minds, you must negotiate and agree as a team on which five items you are going to take along. Again prioritise them, giving 5 points to the most important item.

Remember, the ship is sinking fast!

Operation Abandon Ship Worksheet

The Test!

Well done, you have reached the island and have brought along plenty of tinned food and the five items, namely (list those chosen).

Now, let me ask you some questions:

How are you going to open the tins?

How are you going to cook your food?

How are you planning to collect drinking water?

How are you going to defend yourselves from wild animals?

How will you protect yourselves from bad weather?

A boat crosses the horizon. How are you going to attract its attention?

The boat didn't see you. It is your granddad's birthday and you want to send him birthday greetings. You might even want to send a 'mayday' for help. How will you send your message?

It has now been a few months since the shipwreck and the tins are finished. How will you get food?

A few years have passed. Your message hasn't got through. How can you escape from the island?

Did you take the right items from the list?

In this day and age where everything can be bought precooked from the supermarket and your only worry is how to watch two programmes on different channels at the same time, are you still able to make the right choices?

Can you still survive?

Operation Abandon Ship Worksheet

Operation Abandon Ship Worksheet

Your Choice	Items	Team Choice	Score
	Rope		
	Radio cassette player with batteries		
	Blanket		
	Torch		
	Notebook & pencil		
	Spade		
	Rubber tyre		
	Book of maps		
	Spoon		
	Empty oil-drum		
	Flare		
	Football		
	Empty bottle		
	Sun-cream		
	Compass		
	Magnifying glass		
	Mirror		
	Umbrella		
	Cigarette lighter		
	Plastic bucket		

Operation Op!

Aim **A team-building activity in which the children first have to make their own choice and then come to a shared choice. The choice confronts the children with their own preferences about people.**

Materials **The worksheets and pencils**

Description **The group is presented with a worksheet which places them in a fantasy situation of being the local surgical team at the general hospital. From a list of five people they have to choose one to be operated on.**

Time **15 to 20 minutes**

Guidelines

Hand out the worksheets and read them together. Stimulate them to explain their reasoning. Acknowledge too feelings about the unfairness of the situation.

Anecdotal evaluation

This exercise can actually elicit quite sharp judgements and biases by children. It is important to acknowledge these feelings and explore them instead of becoming judgmental oneself and pushing the nasty feelings away, it is important to remember that:

Every feeling can be accepted.
Not every action can be accepted.

Related activities

The activity *Operation Abandon Ship* is a similar activity but less value-based.

The above activity brings the children in touch with the theme of losses and possibly too, with situations in their own families.

Operation Op! Worksheet

Imagine that you are a group of doctors and surgeons at your local general hospital. Like any doctor you are very pressed for time and there is a long waiting list.

There are five patients waiting for an urgent heart operation. If they do not get it in time they might die. You as a group only have time and money to operate on one of them in the short term. You will have to prioritise!

Turn to the next page for a description of the five patients.

First make your own individual choice, who you would 'rescue' and give the reasons why.

____

____

____

____

____

Then discuss with your team and choose together which person you would rescue as a team. Explain why you as a group came to that conclusion.

____

____

____

____

____

Operation Op! Worksheet

Waiting List for Urgent Heart Operations

Your local family doctor, Mrs Brown.
She has been working in the town for many years.
She is 45. She is married and has three grown-up children.

The Mayor of your town, Mr Green.
He is greatly valued for what he has done for the town: a new leisure centre and the town's own fire brigade. Mr Green is 55, married, but has no children.

The local school crossing patrol lady, Mrs Yellow.
She is well liked by all the children as she always smiles.
Mrs Yellow is 63, widowed and has 12 grandchildren.

The captain of the local football team, Mr Black.
Thanks to him, the local club won most of its matches and was promoted last year. Mr Black is 28, married and has two children in primary school.

One of your teachers, Mrs Red.
She is a very good teacher, but not everybody likes her.
She can be quite firm but always honest. She organises the Christmas show and the summer fair every year.
Mrs Red is 33 and a single parent, she has one daughter in secondary school.

Session advice: 4-8

Themes:
IDENTITY & SELF-ESTEEM
COOPERATION
PROBLEM-SOLVING
EXPRESSION OF FEELINGS
EMPATHY
VERBAL

Rap & Right

Aim — **A playful way to introduce the theme of arguments and get the children to think about the different sides to a story.**

Materials — **The worksheet with the poem, copied for each child.**

Description — **A rap poem is read to the group and then repeated several times while the children act out the different animals.**

Time — **15 to 20 minutes**

Guidelines

Everybody gets a copy of the poem. First it is read together, or by one of the leaders. Then the roles are divided and while acting the characters the group goes through the story again. The children can switch roles various times and repeat the story.

Anecdotal evaluation

Some groups really take to this activity and even want to continue at the next session. If used in a class it might be practised for performance, eg, at the school assembly. Children also take great pleasure in reading the script and as such directing the group.

Related activities

The element of play comes back in *What's my Line?* and more seriously in *What Happens Next?*

The rap poem *Judge too Much!* confronts the listener with other people's situations.

City Dwellers is another rap poem to perform and to encourage children to explore and enjoy their environment.

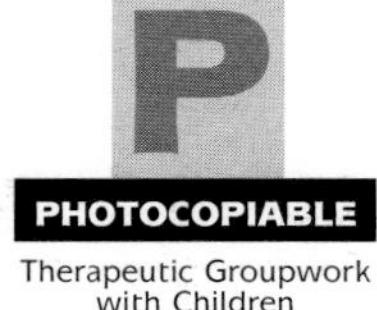

Rap and Right!

I'll tell you a story about a grumpy old bear,
who lived in the woods between here and there.

He ran through the night,
rather short of sight.
He hit a big tree,
and cried 'Oh wee, Oh wee'.

But when the cry died down,
the 'wee' went on.
It was a lion with a crown,
whose head he was standing on.

'Oh you grumpy old bear, get off my head,
You stupid old fool, get off or you'll be dead!'

But the bear crushed the crown
and he pushed the lion down.

It is such a shame,
who is to blame.
It's for you to decide,
who is wrong, who is right!

The bear stamped his feet, just twice more.
Then the lion he escaped with a painful roar.
But the lion took revenge;
he bit the bear in his pants.

'Ouch' cried the bear,
'that's not fair.'

But it's for you to decide,
who is wrong, who is right!

Soon it started to pour down with rain,
big coconuts fell, landing on their brains.
'We're not getting wet, oh wee, oh wee.
Will you stop that now, you scruffy monkey!'

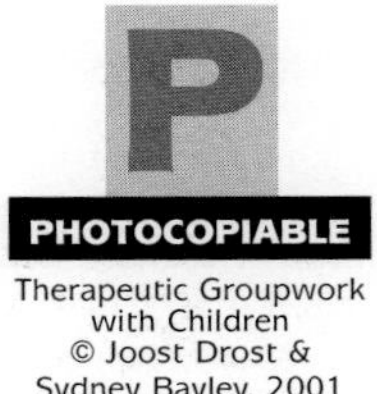

But the monkey wouldn't stop,
and threw stones down on top.
'If you make such a noise in the middle of the night,
being hit with stones just serves you right!'

But it's for you to decide,
who is wrong, who is right!

So the lion and the bear, at the ends of their tether,
could not avoid having to work together.
They chopped the tree down
and with it came the monkey,
who pinched the lion's crown
and he gave it to a donkey.

It's for you to decide,
who is wrong, who is right.

So the lion and the bear they started to pull,
that poor little monkey completely apart.
But the monkey was brave and he stayed rather cool.
He just pointed at the donkey, who looked rather smart.

The donkey then quietly brayed for attention:
'Although famous for being stupid, I wanted
to mention:

Even I can see, if it hadn't been for monkey,
the lion and the bear, wouldn't be friends,
they are now working as a pair
and so the story ends!'

City Dwellers

Themes:
IDENTITY & SELF-ESTEEM
EXPRESSION OF FEELINGS
COOPERATION
VERBAL

Aim — **To encourage children in cities to derive strength from where they live.**

Materials — **Worksheet**

Description — **A guided imagery activity about living in the city, bending under the pressure, discovering the pleasure. A rap poem is read and performed, inviting children to explore and enjoy the world around them.**

Time — **10 to 20 minutes**

Guidelines

Read the poem together and rehearse it. Try to get the rhythm of the rap right, as it will definitely make it more fun to perform. Children can try to memorise different parts to perform together. Invite the children to discover new things through smelling, hearing, seeing and feeling. They can also make up new parts for this rap.

If it is possible, you can also go for a walk and discover new things together.

Anecdotal evaluation

Children take pleasure in performing this type of poem and in adding their own lines.

The art of tuning into the world around you, and being amazed and amused by it, is one of the most important skills in life. This activity could be just the start.

Related activities

Rap and Right and *Judge too Much!* are both poems to perform and some groups and leaders really take to them.

The Horse and *2222!* are both guided imagery activities, trying to stretch and free the children's imagination.

City Dwellers Worksheet

City Dwellers

pressure, pleasure, pressure, pleasure, pressure, pleasure, preasure, spleasure, spreasure, spreash, splash, splash, splash, splash, splash ...

We are walking in the rain
Down the street or down the drain
The city is so grey
I don't know if I want to stay.

There are so many things I have to think about
It is really not safe, playing out
Every place to run around, is taken up by cars
And in the night stupid streetlights hide all my stars.

There is never a moment of fresh air
But nobody seems to ever care
Even when I can see the sun
I don't think the city is much fun
It's like an enormous melting pot
Millions of people, stuffy, hot.

I want to cry, I want to shout
and run far, far away
But then I know, there is no way out
The city and I are here to stay.

Pressure, pressure
Pleasure, pleasure
Splash, splash, splash, splash.

A fantasy is what you need my friend
To bring all this misery to an end
Find the fun in what you see
It is everywhere and it is free.

Find the fun in what you smell
in what a sniff of air can tell.

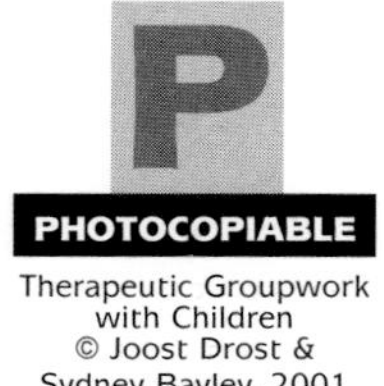

Early in the morning; you are on your way
to another boring schoolday
but sniff like a dog
and even in the city fog
You will find traces
that can put a smile on your faces
A bakery with fresh baked buns
a sweaty person that runs
a lady's sweet perfume
as if a thousand flowers were in bloom
or a winter's breeze of crisp new snow
the smell of coffee from a window.

Splash, splash, splash
Some corners don't smell fresh
they have been used for a dog to poo
or even as a human loo.

I want to cry, I want to shout
and run far, far away
But then I know, there is no way out
The city and I are here to stay.

A fantasy is what you need my friend
To put all this misery to an end
Find the fun in what you see
It is everywhere and it is free.

A taxi-driver half asleep
causing an enormous traffic heap;
an early bird searching through the bins
not for sea-shells but for fish-tins;
a business man, tidy for his daily race
but in one shoe his daughter put a yellow lace;
don't stare at the window cleaner far above your head
just for once please watch his ladder instead.

Find the fun in what you hear
the city becomes music to your ear
the city awakes
with shrieking of the brakes
the wind howling in alleys

the hunger rumbling in bellies
the tapping of the feet
sounds different on a wet street
so do the tyres of a car
you will hear them from afar.

A fantasy is what you need my friend
To put all this misery to an end.
Find the fun in what you see.
It is everywhere and it is free.

Hear the cars and close your eyes
imagine it is a whale that cries;
it is stranded in your road
and needs you to get it afloat.

Look above, there are different rooftops everywhere
they can tell you what kind of people are living there;
some are posh and drink tea from silver cups
some drink beer and get lots of hiccups.
some have aerials, some have dishes
and all the people have blue-sky wishes.

The scent of a tandoori
brings you to a different story
where elephants take you for a ride
you can use their trunk as slide.

Whatever you hear, whatever you see,
whatever you smell, whatever you feel.
Always use a pinch of fantasy
and never be bored again for real.

pressure, pleasure
splash, splash

Task:

Next time when you walk into town, take a moment to stand still and close your eyes, listen, smell and then look, discover the town as if it was your very first time.

Write down some funny facts, write your own poem.

Judge too Much!

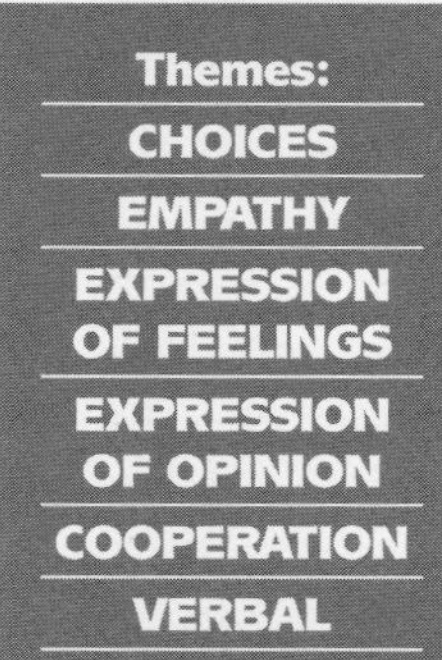

Session advice: 5-9

Themes:
CHOICES
EMPATHY
EXPRESSION OF FEELINGS
EXPRESSION OF OPINION
COOPERATION
VERBAL

Aim — **To help the children reflect on how they see others and empathise when they might hurt or judge others.**

Materials — **Worksheets photocopied for each child**

Description — **A rap poem is read to the group and the children might learn to recite it in chorus. They might also be invited to talk about examples they have come across and to make up their own rap.**

Time — **20 to 30 minutes**

Guidelines

Hand out the rap poem and read it together. Then divide the text and distribute the lines to different groups of people to practice. Be aware that this poem might provoke a lot of feelings as well as instant teasing within the group. There needs to be an existing atmosphere of respect in the group in order to be able to address the feelings within the group.

Anecdotal evaluation

We think that this poem will evoke strong feelings within the group. Be aware that you should not push these feelings away but rather explore them with the group. As with most rap poems the text is sharp as well as funny. Making fun is one of the main driving forces in teasing and bullying. One could discuss what kind of fun is acceptable and when it is goes too far.

Related activities

The activity *Rap and Right* is a more light-hearted rap poem to start with.

Just too much
Judge too much

I am walking down a street.
where the people are pretty neat.

They comb their grass
        with a fine toothbrush.
They polish every pebble
        on their endless garden path.
When it rains, they really loose their brains,
        putting tiny little umbrellas
        on all their rose buds.
If you ask me, well ah,
        I think they're pretty nuts!

Say that again
and I ask you when
You just too much
Do judge too much

I saw a boy
        with his ears sticking out.
There was a storm coming up,
        so I gave him a shout.
'You better lower your sails, mate,
        before it is too late, mate,
Comes galeforce ten,
You are a goner, man!'

Say that again
and I ask you when
You just too much
Do hurt too much

I saw a little girl
        with double glazing on her nose.
'Are you sure' I said,
        'those windows keep the rain out?'
But she stared at me
        and her eyes got wet!

Say that again
and I ask you when
You just too much
Do hurt too much

There was a fine young lass,
    who always plastered her face,
    in a colourful mess,
    a pink and blue disgrace.
'There is no need, I am sure,
    so, what are you renovating for?'
She peeled a layer off
    and showed me her skin.
It was dwindling away,
    frail and thin.

Say that again
and I ask you when
You just too much
Do judge too much

Bodies, Thoughts and Feelings

Session advice: 5-9

Themes:
EXPRESSION OF FEELINGS
IDENTITY & SELF-ESTEEM
SELF-CONTROL
VERBAL

Aim

The aim of this exercise is to help the children to get in touch with and identify their feelings. There is an explicit link in this exercise between how the body feels under certain conditions or circumstances and how this corresponds with thoughts and feelings in the head.

Materials

Worksheet and pencils

Description

A picture of a gingerbread figure is used to allow the children to explore verbal metaphors which use feelings associated with the mind and body. They are encouraged to look at the thoughts and circumstances that go with these feelings.

Time

20 to 30 minutes

Guidelines

Each child is given copy of the gingerbread person on which they can write or draw their answers. Go through the body parts of the gingerbread person one by one, asking questions about the feelings that might go with that part, for example, the head – hot headed.

Let the children give examples of what makes them hot headed. You might start at the top of the body, or the bottom. The worksheet is only a guide to the questions you might ask.

With older children you might decide not to read out the questions but to hand them out (worksheet 3). Children might also be invited to make up their own questions.

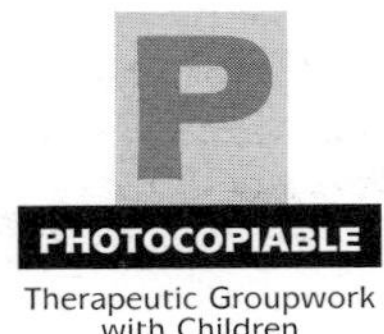

Anecdotal evaluation

Body awareness plays an important role in raising understanding of feelings and emotions. This is especially so for anger. By locating the feeling the person becomes more conscious of what state he is in and will be better able to exert some self-control if he wishes. Gaining this awareness is particularly well facilitated through activities that are fun. The linking of the body to thoughts and circumstances also helps people learn about triggers that induce certain feelings.

Related activities

The guided imagery activities such as *The Horse* and *2222!* use questions that raise awareness of body feelings.

The trust activity *Labyrinth* can be used to explore how the different ways of being guided elicit different feelings in the body.

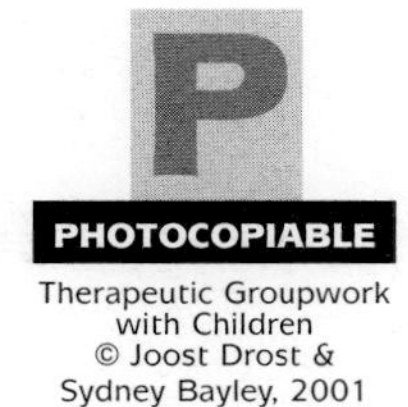

Bodies, Thoughts and Feelings Worksheet 1

Possible questions

1 What makes you hot headed? What makes you heavy headed?

2 What gives you a headache?

3 Does anything make you want to tear your hair out?

4 What makes steam come out of your ears?

5 Does anything make you see red?

6 What makes you blush/go red in the face?

7 What gives you a lump in your throat?

8 What makes you want to sing?

9 What gives you a pain in the neck?

10 Does anything weigh your shoulders down?

11 What makes your chest tight?

12 What makes you heavy hearted? What makes you light hearted?

13 What makes your heart ache? What broke your heart?

14 What makes your stomach go tight?

15 What gives you butterflies in your stomach?

16 Does anyone or anything makes your hands tingle?

17 What makes your legs want to dance?

18 What makes you drag your feet?

19 What makes your toes curl up?

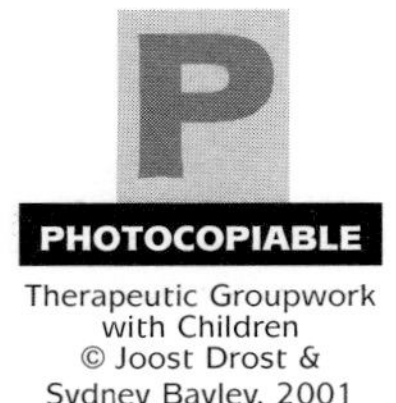

PHOTOCOPIABLE

Bodies, Thoughts and Feelings Worksheet 2

Name

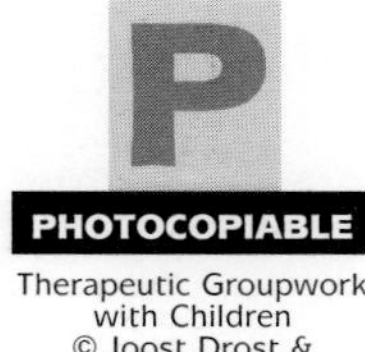

Bodies, Thoughts and Feelings Worksheet 3

Name

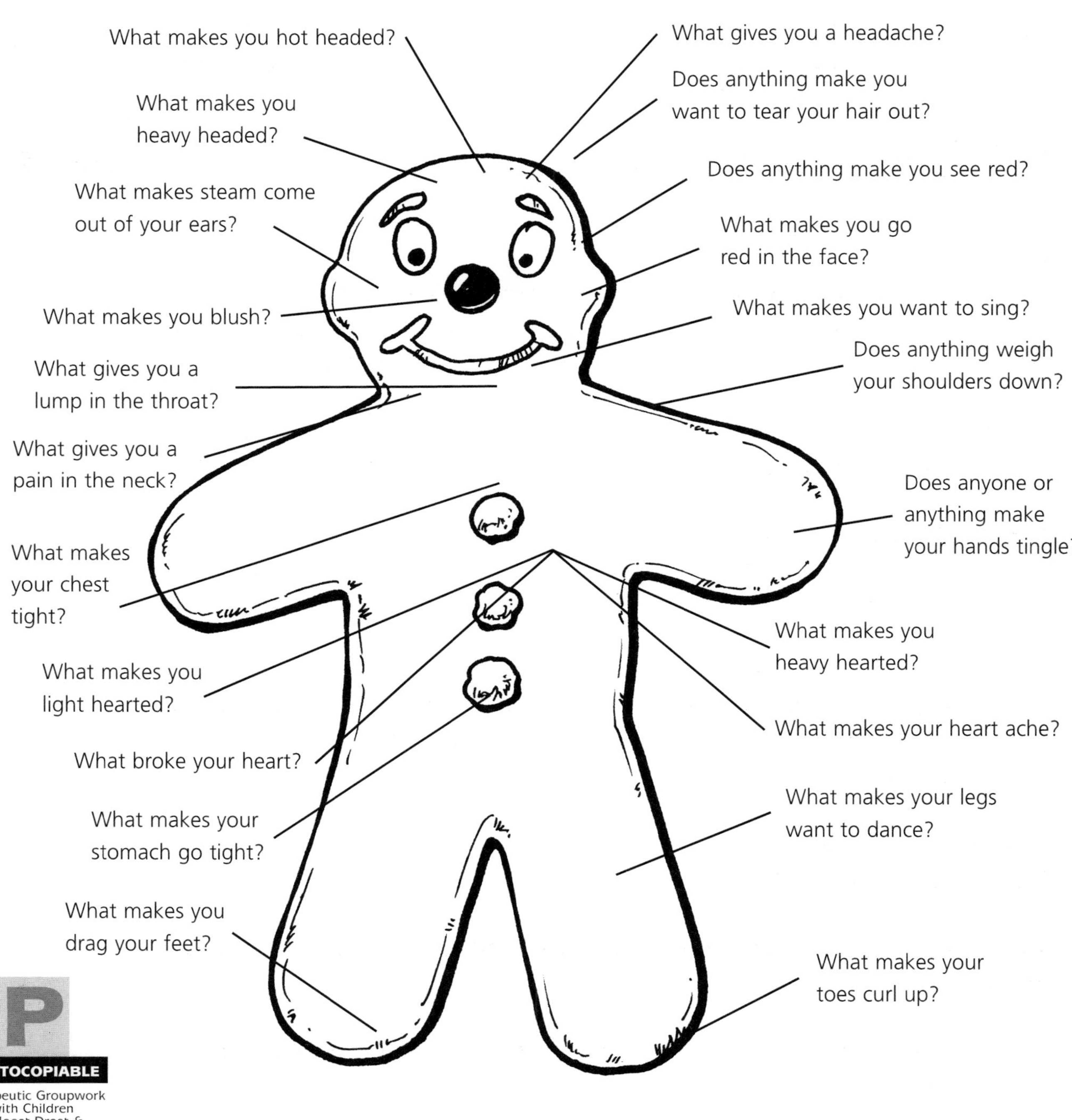

2222!

Aim — **Self-exploration, self-esteem and relaxation while also stretching the imagination.**

Materials — **Worksheet, drawing paper and crayons**

Description — **A guided fantasy in which you take the children into space, to the year 2222 and ask them to design their perfect planet.**

Time — **15 to 20 minutes**

Guidelines
Explain how the exercise works, that you will take the children on a fantasy trip and that they will then have to do a drawing. Hand out the sheets of paper and get the colouring materials ready. Ask them not to use them yet but to listen.

Then read the fantasy, swiftly, carry the children along in the fantasy and when it is finished explain that they have to do a drawing about their perfect planet.

Anecdotal evaluation
This exercise is an easy introduction into guided fantasy work, which might be used in all sorts of ways.

The designing of the planet allows the children to build up a picture of themselves or how they would like their world to be. Sometimes one needs to help a child, as they can be very insecure. It is then important that the child chooses what will be put on the planet.

Related activities
The guided fantasy *The Horse*.

You can also ask children to design their own garden or design an island as a group.

City Dwellers asks the children to fantasise on the basis of what they hear, see and smell in the city.

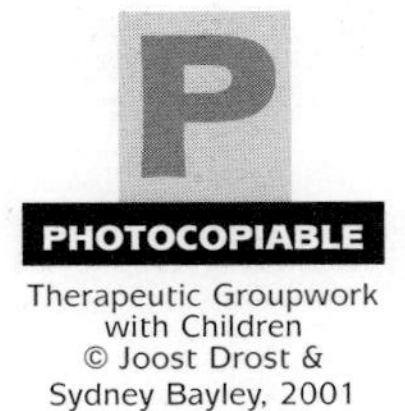

2222! Worksheet

Guided Imagery – Planet 2222

Imagine it is the year 2222, the 22nd day of the 22nd month, because by that year the whole solar system has slowed down. We have been forced to add more months to the year and there was a big dispute whether the extra time should have to be work or leisure time. It took people 22 years to realise that they didn't need to work anyway since all the work was done automatically, everything was done by robots, even the robots were made by robots. People finally have time again to undertake the things they were made for: hunting, exploring, discovering the unknown!

While life is so extremely boring and predictable on earth, deadly controlled in every way, there are the moments when you can whiz away on your space-bikes, flashing off past the moon, gathering star-dust, hopping galaxies, in a whirlpool of light and colours, where everything can happen.

Just see yourselves out there, all alone among the stars, all alone – or do you see other beings? Do you hear other sounds? Do you feel, do you smell something? What did you come across on your journey? Maybe you crash into a steel-blue space-snake, that tries to strangle you but you just about escape, leaving him choking on his own tail.

Or after a cosmic hailstorm you slide into a giant ice-tunnel, faster and faster downwards in a never ending whirlpool and at the end you drop into sheer green bubbling mud, warm and sticky, sweet and juicy. You are definitely drowning when you are pulled out just in time and thrown back into this crazy tumbling adventure by something or someone.

Isn't it marvellous to be exploring again? Take some time, imagine what you encounter next. Imagine that after all the hassle, there is a nice little planet, especially for you, where you can have a rest, where you can feel safe… in fact a planet that you can make your own.

What will you do, what does it look like?

What will be your favourite spot?

What will be your shelter?

The Horse

Themes:
SELF-CONTROL
IDENTITY & SELF-ESTEEM
EXPRESSION OF FEELINGS
NON-VERBAL

Aim — **To increase self-control, self-esteem and relaxation while also stretching the imagination.**

Materials — **Worksheet**

Description — **A relaxing, guided fantasy in which you take the children on a horse ride.**

Time — **10 to 15 minutes**

Guidelines

Ask the children to sit or lie down comfortably, invite them to be by themselves, to close their eyes if they want to and to see this as a time in which they are alone with their fantasy.

Calmly read the guided fantasy. If some children have difficulty joining in, tell them that this is all right, invite them just to listen and respect the others.

Don't be too heavy and serious, after all, fantasy is good fun.

At the end of the fantasy, give the children some time to re-enter the reality of the room.

Anecdotal evaluation

Relaxation with a whole group of youngsters is not always easy and one must judge whether the group is up to it. If they have regular calm moments together, are at ease with one another and make good use of the fantasy activities, this is a good indication of success.

This relaxation exercise was first introduced by a Belgian psychotherapist, Staff Keymeulen (unpublished) who uses relaxation techniques in combination with themes that enhance self-esteem and self-identity.

It is clear that the fantasy of mastering a horse will make children feel better about themselves. It is important that we realise how powerful fantasy can be, and how necessary it is for the growth of children. Plenty of examples can be

seen in everyday life. Joining in with the fantasy and exploring different solutions and story lines can be very helpful, even if they are about the latest craze on television.

Related activities

There is a more simple guided fantasy, *2222!*, that leads up to a drawing activity and can be a good warm-up for this fantasy. *City Dwellers* has been written as guided imagery for children who are faced with living in the city and encourages them to explore and enjoy their environment.

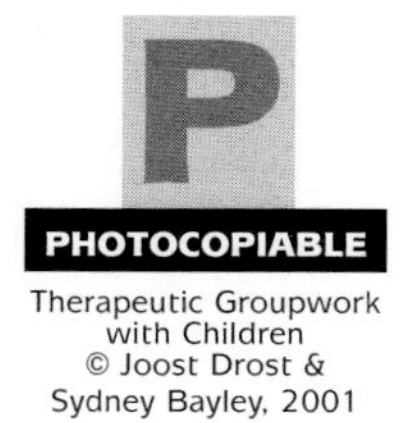

The Horse Worksheet

Relaxation Exercise by Staff Keymeulen

Allow yourself some time off and imagine that you are in front of a gateway, leading to the courtyard of an old farm.

Before you enter the courtyard, you can leave things behind, things you don't need on your day off. You can leave your thoughts in the gateway, every thought, every memory, every worry that you can think of, leave them behind, just here. This will give you more freedom to travel. In this way you can free yourself, you can empty yourself. Just think about everything and then put it in a heap in the gateway. You know that at the end of the day you can always pick them up again, if you feel you need to.

The more you leave behind, the more you can enjoy your day out. Maybe you feel tired. You can also leave your tiredness in the heap. Just enjoy the process of putting everything in the heap for a moment. Carefully observe which parts of your body you leave behind, which parts of your body can relax and sleep, which parts you keep awake, in order to be able to have a nice dream in a sleeping body, a dream that you will remember.

You can dream about the gateway that leads to the farmyard, you can feel it, maybe see it. It is a gateway to freedom, to a place where everything is possible. Just feel it and when you are ready, enter it. Feel that you walk into the courtyard of the old farm, your farm. How is your dream about the courtyard? Is it sunny? Can you see your stables and barns? Where are your living quarters? What are they like? Is there glass in the windows? What kind of walls keep the outside world out? Just look around. Be curious about how your courtyard looks today and feel challenged to go on a wonderful horse ride.

Can you hear the horses in the stables? You can hear their noise. You can smell the horses. You wonder which horse you will ride today. You walk over to the barns. Which horse will you choose? How will you greet your horse? What name will you give it? Notice how it cooperates when you saddle it. Enjoy the movements you make, the care you put into preparing the horse. Can you imagine that the horse feels this as well, that you become friends. Gently you lead it outside, and mount it.

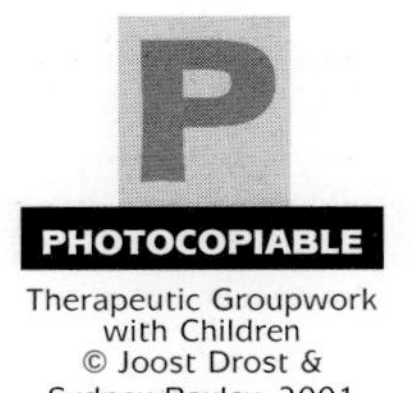

The horse waits, it concentrates, it builds up its strength but waits for your signal. It listens to you. Every movement of the horse is reflected in your body. In this way you get to know your horse. Each of your movements is felt by the horse. In this way it gets to know you. You become closer and closer.

Just wait, find calmness, rest together. Feel how you are seated in the saddle, feel your feet in the stirrups, feel the reins in your hands. Gently but firmly you will lead this horse. Feel how you master the horse in your hands, your legs embrace the horse, its warmth, its strength. Feel how you can master the horse with your words. You decide when to start your journey. Through the fields and through the forest. You decide which way to go, how fast. As you go along you learn to guide the horse, simply by trying to. It doesn't matter if you make mistakes, you can correct them. The horse can make mistakes too and you can teach it. You and the horse get to know each other better.

You ride through the fields on your own horse, at your own pace. You are the master of this horse. Feel how close you get, feel how you sit on its back, feel your legs, your body, your hands holding the reins. Feel the horse breathing. Feel your own breathing. Feel the wind in your face. Together you explore the countryside. It changes. There can be a forest, a forest with beautiful trees and plants. A forest with challenges, obstacles, fallen trees, even hedges that you have to jump. Together with your horse you decide. You know whether you can jump them. You both have the right to refuse. You decide together, you are at one with the horse. Obstacle after obstacle, new challenges. You are invited to do things that you have never done before. Feel the excitement of all the new things that you do. Enjoy it again and again. Feel how you learn, how you are the horse's master, but also how you are at one with it. Feel how the horse enjoys it. Together you play with the challenges. You explore the woods. Some of the obstacles might be too high to jump. Just leave them for another time. You have plenty of time to enjoy things you have never done before. In this way the horse is satisfied, you are satisfied. Whether you are on your own with the horse or whether there are more people in the forest, don't let this disturb you, just enjoy it. Find your way through the forest and when you feel it is time, you can start to make your way back.

Enjoy your journey back. Realise what you have learned from the horse. Feel how it has enjoyed the journey. Feel how you can enjoy everything. You can look at the countryside. You can feel the horse. You can feel your body and at the same time your attention is with the horse. Feel how you are the rider of the horse, feel it in your legs, your knees, your fingers.

You return to the courtyard and gently dismount the horse. You stroke it, you praise it. Keep the feeling of being the master, the rider. Know that you can do it again. You take the saddle off. You groom the horse. Decide whether you will return it to its stable or take it out to the field. Then come back to the courtyard. See the stables, see the barns. You can still feel that you are the rider, all the power and all the skills that you have shown in riding your horse are still with you. They are resting within you. You still feel at one with the horse. With this good feeling, think how you want to do the things that you still have to do. Think what you would like to do in future. Imagine your own future. Be calm and strong, like you were when you were together with the horse.

Think how you can keep this feeling alive. When you slowly, gently come back to this room and wake up again. Keeping this good feeling alive.

Session advice: 6-10

Themes:
LISTENING
PROBLEM-SOLVING
ICE-BREAKER
VERBAL

Robbery

Aim — **To encourage listening and thinking skills.**

Materials — **The story (worksheet), pencil and paper for keeping score.**

Description — **A story about a robbery and questions to help the detective.**

Time — **20 to 25 minutes**

Guidelines

The story is read to the children; they are invited to listen carefully and to take notes, because there will be a quiz afterwards. After the story, the questions are asked and points are awarded for a correct answer. Shouting out is not allowed; hands have to be raised so watch carefully to see who is first.

Anecdotal evaluation

This is a competitive activity which in itself seems to be motivating. It is good fun and makes the children listen hard, even if they appear not to be, and it makes them think.

If there is a lot of competitiveness in the group, which can often lead to physical goading, it is helpful to channel this struggle in more creative ways. By introducing various sorts of competitions everybody might have a chance to do well. Giving continuous positive feedback on cooperative behaviour will gradually shift the focus to working together.

This exercise requires quite a lot of concentration and is not suitable for younger groups.

Related activities

The activities *What's my Line?* and *Empathy Riddles* are very suitable to be used in a competitive and quiz-like form.

PHOTOCOPIABLE

Robbery Worksheet

It was a cold and nasty day. Every now and then there was a cold shower. Only at lunch time the sun broke through – and in the middle of the big city everything happened at lunchtime.

But our story starts early in the morning. John got up at ten to seven, not his normal time. He usually had a lie-in until nine or later because he was out of a job. He hadn't slept very well, he had a terrible cold that kept him awake for most of the night. And on top of that his upstairs neighbour, Lisa, the nice looking girl with long blond hair, had for some reason been doing DIY the whole night long; drilling, hammering and sawing.

John was health conscious, so he had muesli for breakfast but today he ate some raw garlic as well to cure his cold. He looked outside and as it was raining cats and dogs he put on his warm woollen winter jumper, his woollen socks and his green trousers. Then he went out. He had a lot to do that day; first he went to the department store to buy tights.

Upstairs, everything went quiet. Lisa looked satisfied at all the things she had made that night, only she couldn't get the black paint off her hands. Oh gosh, she also had it in her long blond hair. 'We'll think about that later, let's first have a little sleep', so she set her alarm-clock for half-past eleven and dozed off.

Meanwhile John hadn't got much further than the second corner when he bumped into Peter who lived across the road. Or rather he bumped into a mass of paint-pots, brushes, plastic bags and pieces of cloth all dangling from some long wooden poles Peter was balancing on his shoulder. There they sat, both on the pavement, amidst all the pots and brushes. There was even a tape-recorder. 'I am extremely sorry Peter' said John, 'What are you up to?' But Peter seemed uneasy with John's questions and was brusque and rude, 'Look what you've done John, what a mess.' 'But Peter', John stammered, 'it is lucky that only the black tin has sprung open, it could have been worse.' However, Peter only grumbled and pushed John away while he collected his things. He stormed off in his blue jacket and blue jeans without saying another word. John stood feeling helpless, staring at the black spot of paint on the pavement. He was really sorry. Why was Peter avoiding him lately?

He decided to continue on his way to the department store and still arrived too early. It had started to rain and he stood as close as he could with his back to

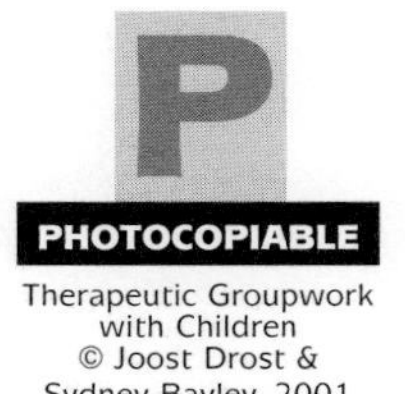

the shop window. When he turned around to see what was in the window he noticed he had left a black stain on the glass. 'Oh no, it is all over my trousers.' He said. The shop opened and John needed some time to find the right pair of tights. He had them packed nicely and asked for a plastic carrier bag. He was happy that he had found the right pair. He looked at his watch. Half-past nine, plenty of time. First he went to the jewellery shop across the street. He stared at the shop window and hesitated about going inside. All the things seemed so expensive. He went in and asked to look at jewellery with jade in it. The shopkeeper showed him some bracelets, rings and earrings. Clumsy, he dropped a ring. He always got nervous in these situations, when he wanted things but could not afford them. He knelt down and picked it up, and gave it back. He made an excuse, 'I'll be back later…' and left the shop. In doing so he almost fell over a tin of paint. What a stupid place to put it. 'Is everybody doing DIY today? This is getting on my nerves! Is it national DIY day?' John wondered whether he should go to the cheaper shops to get cheap jewellery. But no, that would be too obvious. Let's go for something completely different. Three hours until one o'clock, time enough. So off he strolled through record shops, flower shops, toy shops and many other nice shops. By half-past eleven he had what he wanted but also discovered that he had left the bag with tights somewhere. That was stupid, he didn't have enough money to buy new ones. He was pretty tired and cold so he went for a coffee in the department store restaurant. From there he had a view across the street. Whatever was happening there? In the two hours since he had left the jewellery shop somebody had built a kind of puppet theatre in front of it. If this was a kind of advertising stunt, it was a stupid one! It completely blocked the front entrance. That 'somebody' was a clown, who was busy painting the whole thing in bright colours. People were already gathering around. Hopefully this was not going to last too long.

'I must say, things started off really boring that day. I hate it when it rains and somehow even more when it rains in the summer. No real crimes, as the real thieves are sunbathing on sparkling beaches, I bet. It pays to be a thief, not a private investigator, like me… On these days you get stuck with endless requests to listen in on boring telephone conversations. Luckily the sun came out at noon and I decided to go for a stroll in the city. So, what happened there at the jewellery shop, well, there were lots of people around. There was a puppet theatre, how nice. I always get drawn to these things. And the man inside really knew how to make the puppets play. The audience was in his hand, they clapped and cheered. The puppets were good and lively but the most special thing about it was his witty dialogue as well as some very good sound effects. Fascinating. There was even a spell, maybe even as much as five minutes, in which there were no puppets at all to be seen. You could hear them

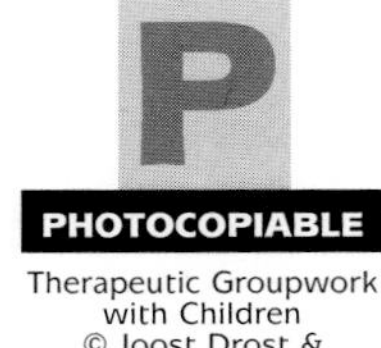

chasing each other up and down stairs, slamming doors and shooting, but his remarks were so funny that you didn't even miss the puppets. The surprise came at the end, as the clock struck one and the puppets had all just reappeared and bowed to the public when they suddenly burst out singing 'Happy birthday to you'. A young lady with short blond hair had just appeared on the scene and started to blush. Out came a very messy clown, his face paint all a blur. He kissed her all over and she was covered in smudged red and white. This man certainly had gone to great lengths for a birthday surprise. Although, I wasn't quite sure if the young lady was as enthusiastic about him as he was about her. Maybe it was just shyness in public. There was another surprise to follow. From the edge of the crowd somebody suddenly shouted 'Help, robbery, help'.

The crowd backed away and a man stumbled forwards, his face covered in black paint and clearly in pain from the paint in his eyes. It was the jeweller. I guided him back inside his shop. His workshop in the back was covered with black paint as well. I went outside again. It had just happened, maybe the robber was still around. In the crowd there were three people with black paint on their hands and I ordered them into the shop. One was the young lady whose birthday it was and appeared to be the shop-assistant, Lisa. Then the blurry clown and puppet-player who said he was called Peter. And finally a young man with a big woollen jumper and a terrible cold, John. The three seemed to know each other, was this all a conspiracy?'

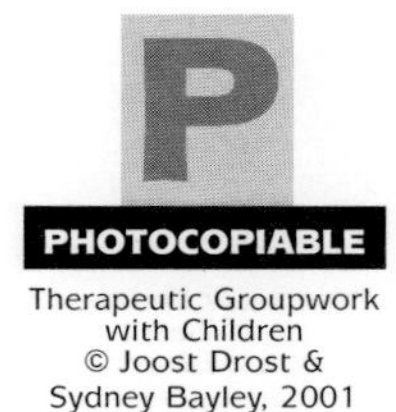

To check the group's listening skills and to prompt their memories for solving the mystery, the teams are quizzed about the story.

Questions

1. What was the weather like that day?
   Cold and nasty with cold showers. Only at lunch time the sun broke through.
2. What time did John get up?
   Ten to seven.
3. What had kept John awake all night?
   He had a terrible cold and his upstairs neighbour, Lisa had been doing DIY all night long.
4. What time did Lisa get up?
   Half-past eleven.
5. What clothes did Peter wear that day?
   A warm woollen winter jumper, his woollen socks and his green trousers.
6. Who lived opposite Peter?
   John.
7. Name four shops that John visited that morning.
   The department store, the jewellery shop, record shops, flower shops, toy shops and other nice shops.
8. Guess why John wanted to buy something that morning.
   It was Lisa's birthday.
9. Why was John nervous in the jewellery shop?
   He wanted to buy things but could not afford them.
10. Name four things that Peter was carrying when John bumped into him.
    Paint pots, brushes, plastic bags, pieces of cloth, tape recorder and wooden poles.
11. John almost came to fall a second time that morning; when and why?
    When he left the jewellery shop and somebody had left a paint tin at the entrance.
12. Where was the jewellery shop?
    Opposite the department store restaurant.

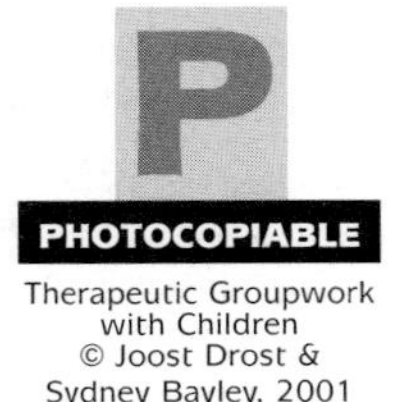

13 What did John see when he went for a cup of coffee?
Somebody had build a puppet theatre in front of the jewellery shop.

14 Why did the private investigator go into town?
Because he was bored.

15 What was so fascinating about the puppet show?
The witty dialogue and good sound effects; there was even a spell of five minutes during which the puppets could only be heard but not seen.

16 How did the puppet show end?
The puppets all started singing 'Happy Birthday' when Lisa arrived.

17 Why did the private investigator select Lisa, John and Peter to come in?
They all had black paint on their hands.

The teams now each have a chance to ask a question of the shopkeeper.

The shopkeeper reports that he saw very little. Busy in his workshop, he didn't notice anybody coming in as the noise from the puppet show was coming through the open door and as he looked up he saw a person with tights over his or her head, maybe a woman as locks of blond hair were still visible. But then he was blinded by the paint and was pushed down by something; he thought it was a gun. The robber took just a few, but very valuable, diamonds.

The private investigator has one final clue:

'I found a bag from the department store containing a new pair of nice tights. Apart from the paint in the workshop there was also a vague imprinted stain on the carpet in the shop which caught my attention. I then discovered some long blond hairs with white stains on them, but they weren't proper paint stains.'

Each team gets a chance to explain who did the robbery.

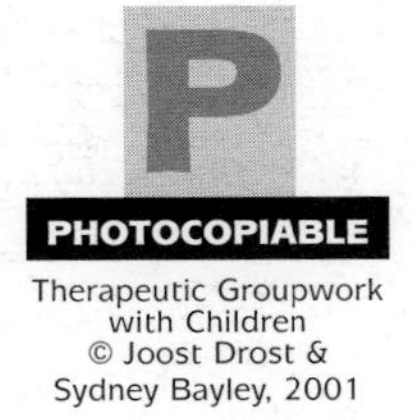

Part III

PART III

APPENDIXES

Develop Your Own Activities

Although this book is designed to be ready for use, we would like to emphasise that these kind of groups require improvisation and flexibility. You have to be able to change the programme and use a pick-and-mix approach to suit your particular group. You may sometimes need to invent new activities that will address particular experiences of the group.

Following are some suggestions for designing new activities and some exercises to stimulate you to begin.

How do you know that you need to design a new activity?

You might run special groups that require special activities. In a school setting this could, for example, focus on bullying and making friends, disability or following a traumatic event.

In the clinical setting one could think of running more specific groups, for example focusing on extreme shyness, anxiety, soiling or compulsive-obsessive problems. This will require looking at some of the literature for the specific problems and translating the therapeutic techniques into group activities.

Note that in the life of a general group you could also perceive that the group is not yet ready to move on to a more difficult stage such as working with emotions or problem solving. You will have to design extra activities around listening, turn-taking or making choices. More specific problems might also arise in the group. For example, there might be an ongoing battle amongst the children to decide who is the strongest.

What do you need to think about when designing an activity?

You must determine the main aim of the new activity. You need to decide the level of the group and whether it should be a verbal or non-verbal activity. Should it be more of an individual experience, does it have to be paired work or a whole group activity? What are the most important skills you want to encourage, what are the themes and processes that you want to stimulate?

Establish what is important to the group

The children in one particular group we ran – quite young in age – were always making dens out of the beanbags. Therefore, we decided to develop an activity around the den and often ended up having more serious discussions sitting all together in the tiny den.

Some groups are forever trying to establish a pecking order. We sometimes introduce wrestling, but we also try to think about other activities which would help to show each person's strengths and skills. Children are often used to competitiveness and it can be used as a motivational technique. Many of the activities can be used in a competitive way with only slight adjustments. However, we make sure that we start with individual competition but then shape this into paired and group competition and eventually would have whole group activities where the children would have to improve themselves as a group. In this way working together becomes more important than being competitive with each other.

One golden rule we always follow is that more of the same is often the best solution.

If there is a lot of chaos, actually make chaos the focus of your next activity and let the children cope with it, let them find their own way out of it. Equally, if there is a lot of shouting, make it into a game and challenge the children to calm themselves down.

Remember that the children need to be able to experience different emotions and behaviours and need to learn not to get stuck in them but to move on and make sense of their experiences.

It is not always necessary to discuss experiences, to over-empathise and to dig up the roots of the feelings. It is often enough just to give the children a chance to express themselves and to acknowledge what they have to say. If every personal statement a child makes is followed by a lot of questions and empathy, some children will stop expressing themselves. They may experience all the attention as negative, while other children will start to express themselves constantly as they experience the attention as a reward. Every group is unique, and you must tune in to their individual needs.

Keep the activities simple

Activities should always be kept simple. After all they are just a means in the group process and they should not be an end in themselves. In any case, children do not need a lot to get them going.

Following are ten ideas, to stimulate you when designing activities.

1. Start with the activity *Boxes and Bellies*. How can you turn this exercise into a whole-group activity, in which everybody needs to work together at the same time? Think too about three other ways in which the boxes can be used afterwards; one involving problem solving, another about expression and one concerning endings.

2. Think about four common playground games which you might use in the group to help listening skills and self-control.
3. Design an activity in which the children have to guess each other's facial expressions.
4. Design an activity around fashion and self-identity for children aged eight to ten.
5. Design an activity around toys and self-identity for the younger children, aged five to seven.
6. One of the children in the group keeps using a lot of swear words. This may just be a bad habit or an attempt to impress others, or a means of expressing his discontent about the group. Design an activity which helps the group to explore different ways to tackle this issue.
7. Design activities which help multi-racial groups to explore their differences and to help the children to build their self-esteem.
8. Christmas is coming and the group finds it hard to concentrate. Can you design an activity around Christmas focusing on choices and problem-solving. This may be along the lines of *Operation Op!*.
9. Children love to have the chance to use the black- or white-board. In fact, they cannot leave it alone if you try to run your group in a classroom. Design a verbal and a non-verbal activity, using the board, focusing on cooperation.
10. Ask the children to help you to develop an activity focused on finding alternative solutions in difficult situations, based on their favourite television programmes.

There are no right solutions to these suggestions. They are only there to help you to get started.

The same goes for the groups themselves. You need to get started. It will not be perfect; it never will be, but along the way you will improve.

APPENDIX 1

Bubble Gum Guy

A synopsis

This book was especially written for the groups. It deals in a metaphorical way with self-control and self-esteem. Every chapter addresses part of the therapeutic process.

Chapter one introduces Guy, a boy born with a irremovable piece of bubble gum in his mouth. At first it makes him extra cute, but when Guy cannot get what he wants, he gets angry and the bubble explodes and covers everybody in sticky stuff. People get annoyed with the way Guy gets angry and his classmates take pleasure in getting Guy to explode. Guy feels very much on his own. This is the recognition of the problem phase. There is no magic solution, no pill or knife that can remove the bubble gum. Then Guy meets an old pearl diver who offers to teach him to dive, which requires a good breathing control, and thus bubble control. This indicates that change can be achieved, not by magic, but possibly with the help of an understanding adult.

Chapter two tells how Guy already feels better with the prospect of going to the old pearl diver in the summer. He explodes less often. Both his teachers and other pupils at school still judge him on his old reputation and even if he doesn't explode he is criticised for daydreaming.

Only his parents start to understand him, support him and help to prepare him for his course in pearl diving.

As the moment draws nearer Guy starts to doubt himself and his bubble explodes more often again. People tell his parents that they knew that Guy could not change.

Guy's parents stick with him and give him a pocket knife for his expedition. This shows Guy that his parents really trust him.

This chapter indicates that just the finding of the source of help is half the solution, but that the world will keep judging you on your old reputation. It emphasises how important it is to have your parents' trust.

Chapter three describes how Guy arrives at the old man's cottage. Horrible weather prevents them from diving the first few days and all they do is repair the boats. Guy becomes very insecure at this stage. It is hard work but nothing seems to change. But instead of his bubble exploding, Guy starts to cry. The old man praises him, and tells him to listen to his confusion.

The next day they go out to dive. Guy cannot wait to explore the yacht and almost drowns. All the old man does is speak calmly to him, every time he surfaces totally out of breath. Words about listening to himself, to his fears and his hopes.

This chapter indicates that overcoming your problem is hard work, which you have to do yourself. Others can only give you guidance. It also encourages the child to find the solution within himself.

Chapter four is a moment of celebration, harvesting what has been learned.

Guy hunts for a treasure in the rock pools and finds a magic treasure. They build a campfire and the old man tells his life story. They swim in a fluorescent sea.

This part helps to consolidate and deepen the good feeling within the child.

Chapter five is about ending. Guy is anxious about going back home, and wants a real treasure to take home with him. Guy and the old man go on a final journey to an underwater cave. Just as Guy begins to panic they find an air bubble, but no real treasure. Guy gets only a pebble to remind him of the week with the old man.

When Guy returns home, it is the same old world, still expecting him to explode. However, Guy has changed and he makes one more journey to the sea to prove to himself that he can also do it on his own.

This chapter helps the children to prepare for the ending of the group and encourages them to hold on to the changes within themselves, to be happy with themselves.

Bubble Gum Guy by Joost Drost was published by Bloomsbury in 1997 and is available from bookshops, ISBN 0 7475 3125 0, alternatively, contact the author on drost-education@lineone.net.

Pre-treatment Questionnaire

______________________________ will be taking part in a group this term. We would be grateful if you would complete this form. We will send you a similar form at the end of the group so that we can measure outcomes.

Please rate the pupil on the following measures *in the last two weeks:*
(0 is the worst you have experienced in your teaching career and 10 is the best)

1 Standard of behaviour within the classroom 0 1 2 3 4 5 6 7 8 9 10

2 Social relationships with peers 0 1 2 3 4 5 6 7 8 9 10

3 Relationships with adults 0 1 2 3 4 5 6 7 8 9 10

4 Attention to task 0 1 2 3 4 5 6 7 8 9 10

5 Self-esteem 0 1 2 3 4 5 6 7 8 9 10

Any further comments

Signed ______________________________ Date __________________

Position ______________________________

Post-treatment Questionnaire

_____________________________ took part in a group last term. We would be grateful if you would complete this form so that we can measure outcomes.

Please rate the pupil on the following measures *in the last two weeks:*
(0 is the worst you have experienced in your teaching career and 10 is the best)

1	Standard of behaviour within the classroom	0	1	2	3	4	5	6	7	8	9	10
2	Social relationships with peers	0	1	2	3	4	5	6	7	8	9	10
3	Relationships with adults	0	1	2	3	4	5	6	7	8	9	10
4	Attention to task	0	1	2	3	4	5	6	7	8	9	10
5	Self-esteem	0	1	2	3	4	5	6	7	8	9	10

Any further comments

Signed ______________________________ Date ________________

Position ______________________________

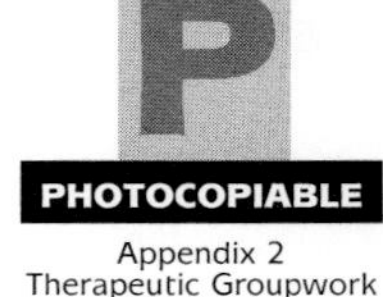

Parent's Treatment Questionnaire

Guidelines for using the following questionnaire.

In our service we discuss with parents whether or not they want their child to participate in the group. At this stage we ask them, with their child, to identify three areas in which they want to see an improvement. We will help them to formulate these focus points in a positive statement, for example, 'What do you wish your child would do more of?' instead of 'What do you wish your child would stop doing?'.

These statements are used in the pre- and post-treatment questionnaire.

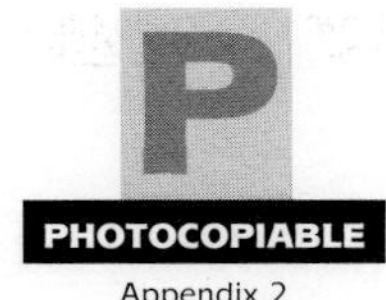

Pre-treatment Questionnaire

We would be grateful if you could complete this form. We will be giving you another form at the end of the group sessions in order to measure outcomes.

Please rate your child on a scale from 0 (which is the worst it has ever been) to 10 (which is the best it could be) on the following statements. Circle one number only for each statement.

1 ____

0 1 2 3 4 5 6 7 8 9 10

2 ____

0 1 2 3 4 5 6 7 8 9 10

3 ____

0 1 2 3 4 5 6 7 8 9 10

Signed ____________________________ Date ________________

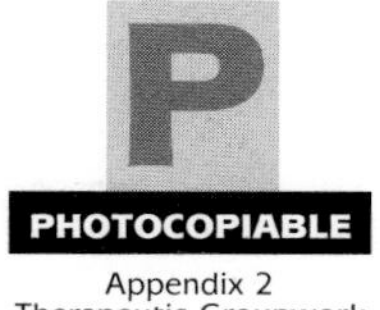

PHOTOCOPIABLE

AN EXAMPLE OF A COMPLETED PARENT'S QUESTIONNAIRE

Pre-treatment Questionnaire

We would be grateful if you could complete this form. We will be giving you another form at the end of the group sessions in order to measure outcomes.

Please rate your child on a scale from 0 (which is the worst it has ever been) to 10 (which is the best it could be) on the following statements. Circle one number only for each statement.

1 To get on well with his siblings and classmates

0 1 2 (3) 4 5 6 7 8 9 10

2 Not to lose his temper so quickly

0 (1) 2 3 4 5 6 7 8 9 10

3 To feel better about himself and be happy

0 1 (2) 3 4 5 6 7 8 9 10

Signed ______________________ Date ______________

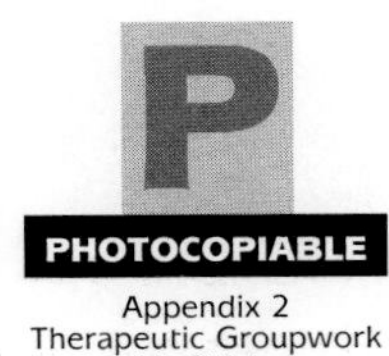

Post-treatment Questionnaire

We would be grateful if you could complete this form. We will compare this form with the one you completed at the start of the group sessions in order to measure outcomes.

Please rate your child on a scale from 0 (which is the worst it has ever been) to 10 (which is the best it could be) on the following statements. Circle one number only for each statement.

1 ____

0 1 2 3 4 5 6 7 8 9 10

2 ____

0 1 2 3 4 5 6 7 8 9 10

3 ____

0 1 2 3 4 5 6 7 8 9 10

Signed ______________________ Date ______________

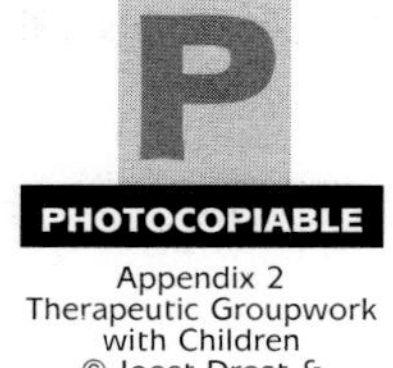

Information Leaflet for Referrers

Short-Term Therapy Group for Children aged 8–11

The Child & Family Consultation Service based in ________________ will run a short-term therapy group in the ___________________ term (20____), for children in the above age group.

The group will be open to children who experience emotional and behavioural difficulties.

Aims & Principles

- We aim to boost the children's **self-esteem**, both as individuals as well as in social situations. We will provide them with consistent, positive reinforcement and focus on their individual qualities and their social qualities.
- We aim to increase their **self-control**. We will reflect on their behaviour openly and invite alternative solutions.
- We aim to encourage them **to be in touch with the present**. We will help them to reflect on their own feelings, beliefs and behaviour and encourage them to make active choices and not just to react. In this way they will also develop their own sense of direction and a positive sense of control.

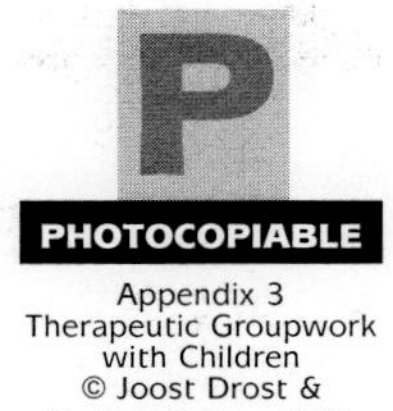

- We aim to increase their **behavioural repertoire**, in order for them to be able to choose more acceptable and effective behaviour, whether to express their feelings or to achieve their goals.
- We aim to increase their **ability to process and reflect upon their own feelings and thoughts**.

Set Up

In this group therapy we will focus on working in the present. We will offer various activities as well as non-structured group time, in which the children can experience, experiment and reflect.

The activities will cover story-telling, games, drama, drawing, modelling, trust-building exercises and both structured and free discussions.

There will be a maximum of 6 children in the group.

There will be two group leaders, who will guide the children through a number of exercises and experiences and will endeavour to reflect a role model of positive communication, constructive feedback and individual responsibility.

The therapy sessions will last for 75 minutes and there will be 10 weekly sessions.

For more information please contact ______________________________

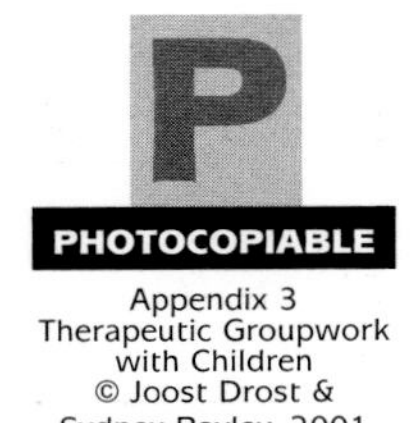

APPENDIX 4

Table of Activities and Themes

Activities	Age	Listening	Empathy	Trust	Ice-Breaker	Identity & Self-Esteem	Self-Control	Problem-Solving	Choices	Expression of Feelings	Expression of Opinion	Endings & Losses	Cooperation	Verbal	Non-Verbal	Session	Page
Be a Tree	5 to 7			✓			✓						✓		✓	1-5	56
Binary Choices	5 to 7				✓	✓			✓						✓	1-3	66
Bodies, Thoughts and Feelings	8 to 11					✓	✓			✓				✓		5-9	170
Boxes and Bellies	5 to 11			✓			✓						✓		✓	2-5	75
Breathing	8 to 11						✓								✓	1-2	121
Breathing for Diving	8 to 11						✓								✓	all	125
Campfire	5 to 11	✓	✓	✓		✓				✓	✓			✓		7-10	114
Chinese Whispers	5 to 11	✓					✓						✓	✓	✓	2-4	89
Circle	5 to 11			✓			✓						✓		✓	4-9	85
City Dwellers	8 to 11					✓				✓			✓		✓	4-8	163
Climbing Up or Down the Tree	5 to 7			✓	✓	✓									✓	all	52
Den, The	5 to 7			✓		✓			✓						✓	3-10	64

Activities	Age	Listening	Empathy	Trust	Ice-Breaker	Identity & Self-Esteem	Self-Control	Problem-Solving	Choices	Expression of Feelings	Expression of Opinion	Endings & Losses	Cooperation	Verbal	Non-Verbal	Session	Page
Draw a Tree	5 to 7			✓			✓						✓		✓	1-3	55
Empathy Riddles	5 to 11	✓	✓							✓			✓	✓		3-9	106
End Game	5 to 11		✓	✓		✓				✓	✓	✓	✓	✓		10	118
Families	5 to 11	✓				✓				✓				✓	✓	2-4	72
Favourite Animal	5 to 11			✓		✓				✓	✓				✓	3-8	87
Feedback Certificates	5 to 11					✓						✓		✓		10	120
Four Corners of the Room	5 to 11					✓	✓			✓					✓	4-8	112
Funny Walks	5 to 11	✓		✓		✓	✓								✓	4-9	83
Group Tree, The	5 to 7					✓						✓		✓		9-10	57
Horse, The	8 to 11					✓	✓			✓					✓	5-9	177
How Do you Do?	8 to 11	✓			✓									✓	✓	1-2	127
Judge too Much	8 to 11		✓						✓	✓	✓		✓	✓		5-9	167
Labyrinth	5 to 11		✓	✓			✓						✓		✓	3-6	81
Losses	5 to 11	✓		✓		✓				✓				✓	✓	8-9	115

Activities	Age	Listening	Empathy	Trust	Ice-Breaker	Identity & Self-Esteem	Self-Control	Problem-Solving	Choices	Expression of Feelings	Expression of Opinion	Endings & Losses	Cooperation	Verbal	Non-Verbal	Session	Page
		Themes															
Magic Box	5 to 11					✓				✓	✓			✓		3-10	91
Mirroring	5 to 11	✓		✓											✓	2-5	74
Name Game, Web	5 to 11	✓			✓											1-2	50
Operation Abandon Ship	8 to 11	✓						✓	✓		✓		✓	✓		3-7	151
Operation Op!	8 to 11	✓							✓		✓	✓	✓	✓		4-8	157
Opposite Sides of the Room	5 to 7		✓	✓			✓			✓	✓				✓	2-5	68
Puppet Play	5 to 7							✓		✓	✓		✓			5-9	62
Puppets	5 to 7					✓				✓	✓		✓			all	60
Rap and Right	8 to 11		✓			✓		✓	✓	✓			✓	✓		4-8	160
Rescue Operation	5 to 11			✓						✓			✓		✓	3-6	84
Robbery	8 to 11	✓			✓			✓						✓		6-10	182
Sad Tears, Happy Tears	5 to 11		✓							✓				✓		4-8	93
Sentence Completion	8 to 11		✓			✓				✓	✓			✓		3-7	137
Situations	8 to 11					✓		✓	✓		✓			✓		4-8	147

Activities	Age	Themes: Listening	Empathy	Trust	Ice-Breaker	Identity & Self-Esteem	Self-Control	Problem-Solving	Choices	Expression of Feelings	Expression of Opinion	Endings & Losses	Cooperation	Verbal	Non-Verbal	Session	Page
Snuggles and Grizzles	5 to 11			✓		✓			✓	✓				✓		4-8	95
Statues	5 to 11			✓			✓	✓					✓		✓	3-9	76
Ten Ways to Walk the Room	5 to 7			✓		✓				✓					✓	7-9	70
Volcano	5 to 11			✓						✓			✓		✓	4-9	86
What Happens Next?	8 to 11					✓	✓	✓		✓	✓			✓		4-8	139
What's my Line?	5 to 11	✓						✓		✓					✓	3-9	99
2222!	8 to 11					✓	✓			✓					✓	5-9	175

APPENDIX 5

References

Bion WR, 1962, *Learning from Experience,* Tavistock, London.

Drost JSM, 1997, *Bubble Gum Guy,* Bloomsbury Publishers, London.

Dwivedi KN (ed), 1993, *Group Work with Children and Adolescents, A Handbook,* Jessica Kingsley Publishers, London and Bristol, Pennsylvania.

Foulkes SH, 1975, *Group-analytic Psychotherapy, Methods and Principles,* Gordon and Breach Publishers Ltd, London.

Lewin R 1952, *Field Theory in Social Science*, Tavistock, London.

Mosley J, 1996, *Quality Circle Time in the Primary Classroom*, Learning Development Aids, London.

Rogers CR, 1961, *On Becoming a Person,* Houghton Mifflin Company, Boston.

Slavson SR, 1979, *Dynamics of Group Psychotherapy,* Jason Aronson, New York.

Yalom E, 1970, *The Theory and Practice of Group Psychotherapy,* Basic Books, New York.

APPENDIX 6

An invitation

Promoting positive mental health in schools can be done in various ways; by running groups and circle time, by introducing activities that stimulate personal growth, by having courses and staff support, even in the way we design and furnish our buildings.

Central to all this is that we as people have a sense of being in control, whether we are teachers, pupils, parents or professionals in the helping agencies.

This book tries to bring across some basic principles, attitudes and a bag full of activities.

In order to start to own this process, to start to feel in control yourself, we would like to invite you to start using the book and also to expand on it. Send us your experiences and new activities.

We envisage a database of activities, which could also be integrated into National Curriculum targets in the UK and could be searched by using themes, subject and age, to assist in teaching.

This project will be supported by a future website. It is in its early stages and simply has to start growing. This book is hopefully only a start of something we will share and own together.

Please send your responses to

Joost Drost
Clinical Psychologist
CFCS, Stanwell House, Stanwell Street
Colchester, CO2 7DL
United Kingdom

or e-mail drost-education@lineone.net